I Met the MASTER... I Read the BOOK

A comprehensive mission handbook for the local church

by
V.E. Maybray

I Met the Master...I Read the Book

Copyright © 1999 Virgil Maybray

ISBN: 0-7392-0226-X

Printed in the USA by

MORRIS PUBLISHING

3212 East Highway 30 • Kearney, NE 68847 • 1-800-650-7888

Table of Contents

Introducing V.E. Maybray

The Rev. V.E. Maybray, an elder in the Western Pennsylvania Annual Conference, has served 32 years in the local church pastorate. Very active in conference board and agencies (many of them involving missions and evangelism), he has consistently called our church to higher aims in evangelism and devotion to evangelical missions. In addition to his ministry within denominational channels, he has served on campmeeting and Ashram boards, and for 40 years has conducted evangelistic meetings within the United States and overseas.

The Mission Society for United Methodists is particularly indebted to Virgil. As executive secretary of the Evangelical Missions Council (1976-1984), he helped lay the groundwork for the Mission Society. Later, he became its founding vice president for mission development and played a role in the founding of the Evangelical Methodist Church of Paraguay, with which the Mission Society now partners. Many of our supporting churches, former and present missionaries, and even staff personnel who have come to the Mission Society are testament to Virgil's passion and gift for mobilizing individuals and churches for missions. As mission representative, Virgil continues to motivate and equip congregations to reach outside themselves—to offer Christ to the world.

In 1998 the Rev. Maybray was awarded the Foundation for Evangelism's Harry Denman Award, which recognizes and honors pastors and laypersons who are "doing the vital work of responsible evangelism in ways that are in keeping with history and tradition." This is a well-placed honor for a man who—like the great Methodist missionary statesman John R. Mott—earnestly believes that "the primary work of the church is to make Jesus Christ known and obeyed and loved throughout the world."

This handbook has been a long time in the making, and represents many years of prayer, experience, and deep devotion to the local church. It provides practical ideas and tried-and-true strategies for involving your congregation in missions. As you read, may God stir in your heart an even greater passion to make Christ known.

Working with you for the world,

Dr. Alvern L. Vom Steeg
President of The Mission Society for United Methodists

Chapter 1

Prayer: The Cornerstone, Keystone and Capstone of Missions

In this section we will deal with the paramount importance of prayer in the mission outreach of the Church. Honoring the prayer request of Jesus, how to pray for missionaries and helps that are available for us to pray for effectively and intelligently. A later chapter will deal with Prayer and the Missions Conference.

Paul said, in I Timothy 2:1,3,4,8; *I urge, then, First of all, that requests, prayers, intercession and thanksgiving be made for everyone...This is good, and pleases God our Savior, who wants all men to be saved and to come to a knowledge of the truth...I want men everywhere to lift up holy hands in prayer...*

On my desk I have a bronze plaque on which are inscribed three words, NOTHING BEFORE PRAYER. Obviously, it has a double edged meaning. It means, do nothing before praying. It also means that nothing, significant, happens until or unless we pray. Therefore, I place this chapter on prayer at the very beginning because prayer is our most important contribution and exercise in missions. Sam Kamaleson, long time Vice President of World Vision, International has said, "Universally, the concern for missions starts with prayer."

This is true, first of all, because of the very nature of prayer. It is one of the primary means by which we discover the will of God for our mission endeavor and activity. And, we desperately need His guidance for our efforts so that we do not dissipate our energies and resources on things that will have only a minimal result.

Secondly, it is the one way we can influence the world without ever leaving our bedroom or study. We hear a great deal about satellite communication these days; instantaneously beaming a message from one spot on the globe to some other spot halfway around the world. The Christian Church has had satellite communication from the very beginning. We can beam our message to the Throne where it is unscrambled, interpreted and energized and beamed back to earth to affect and influence our ministry for Christ around the world. To this end we would highly recommend Wesley L. Duewel's book, written several years ago, *Touch The World Through Prayer*.

Finally, and perhaps most importantly, we place prayer first because it is the recognition of our total and absolute dependence on Him for accomplishing of His purpose in the world. This is a case of tapping into our power source. We need to deal with the mechanics of missions, "How To", certainly that is necessary, but we need something to energize the whole thing and prayer is that energizer.

Prayer is the means by which we find guidance, where we fellowship with other world Christians, where we enter into and begin to understand the heart of God for the world.

Now, the question is, "How, and for what shall we pray?"

I. We Need to Pray for the Church's Obedience!

Those who are regular users of the *Global Prayer Digest*, published by the US Center for World Missions, know how often the phrase, "Pray For the Church's Obedience", appears. Jesus has issued a command. We call it the Great Commission which we generally assume was issued to all the disciples. There were no exceptions or exclusions and, to the best of our knowledge, has never been rescinded. Therefore, we need to pray that the Lord will awaken the Church to her primary task—we have no other! All other things which the Church does, however good they may appear to be, if they detract from, or do not contribute to, the fulfillment of our task are a tragic waste of time, effort and resources and may very well be an affront to our Lord. What He wants is obedience, not feverish activity.

Now, in order to do this, the Church must take seriously the prayer request of Jesus. In Matthew 9:37-38 He says to His disciples: *The harvest is plentiful but the workers are few. Ask the Lord of the harvest, therefore, to send out workers into His harvest field.*

How often do we hear people pray for harvesters to be raised up? How seldom is this the burden of the prayer life of the Church! If your experience has been anything like mine, you have discovered that in today's church most praying seems to be for physical healing. We take the prayer requests of members of our church more seriously than we do the prayer request of Jesus. How can we remedy this?

1. When prayer requests are being asked for we might stand up and say, "In the Name of Jesus, or in behalf of Jesus, I request that we pray for God to send forth laborers." God has been speaking to me about this, that I might muster enough courage to stand some morning in the worship service, when prayer requests are being asked for and make this one. I wonder what might happen? Would there be a moment of

embarrassed silence? Would the preacher clear his throat and grope for something to say? Would there be a weak or enthusiastic response?

2. We could ask the pastor to include this in his morning prayer from time to time.

3. We could urge the various prayer groups of the church to make this a regular prayer concern.

4. We might do a little research on how long it has been since our church has produced a missionary or how many it has produced during the years of its existence. We could share this information with the church to help motivate them to pray for harvesters.

For example, the organization called, Advancing Churches in Mission Commitment tells us that there are about 335,000 Christian Churches in America. There are about 40,000 career missionaries out under all boards and agencies (this is not counting short term missionaries). That is about one missionary for every eight churches. What is happening to the other seven? Surely every Church ought to be able to produce at least one missionary!

5. We could have a Harvester Dedication Sunday when parents and grandparents were invited to publicly lay their children and grand children on the altar of God's love and promise to pray that they might hear the call of God to full-time service in His harvest field. I heard of a service where the people were asked to stand and publicly say "Lord, I give you my son or daughter (naming the child) for service in Your Kingdom." We might consider rewriting the Service For Baptism or Dedication so that it includes a sentence to the effect that this child is hereby dedicated to God for service in His Kingdom as a Harvester. We could then ask the parents to covenant to pray for their child that they would consider missions as a life option.

6. We could set, as a part of our Missions Conference, a personnel goal. This would be more important than a financial or Faith Promise goal. It might even make the Faith Promise goal easier to reach.

For example, I was in a little church in south central Michigan and they had set a Faith Promise goal of $17,000 and a Personnel Goal of two persons in full time Christian service. I returned to that church several years later and their Faith Promise goal was now $36,000 and twenty persons in some kind of short term or full time service.

7. Finally, we could, with Isaiah, pray, "Here am I Lord, send me!" You remember that immediately after our Lord said to His disciples, "Pray, that the Lord of the harvest will send forth laborers" that *they*

were sent forth. Those who did the praying did the going! Perhaps this is what makes us so reluctant to pray for harvesters. We have a feeling that we might become the answer to our prayers!

II. You Can't Pray for God to Raise up Harvesters Without Praying for the Harvesters

World Intercessors of OMS, International says, "Most Christians believe in the importance of prayer but missionaries survive by it." Everyone of us has heard some missionary tell of miraculously getting through some extremely difficult situation only to later learn that some saint back home had been strangely led to pray for him or her at that exact time. Betty Constance of the *Christian and Missionary Alliance* calls them her Co-laborers.

Certainly it is significant to note how frequently Paul, in writing to the churches requests prayer. In Romans 15:30 he says, *I urge you, brothers, by our Lord Jesus Christ and by the love of the Spirit, join me in my struggles by praying to God for me.* Similar passages can be found in Ephesians 6:18-20, Colossians 4:2-4, I Thessalonians 5:25, II Thessalonians 3:1 and Hebrews 13:18-19.

Virtually every mission board or agency puts out a leaflet telling you why and how to pray for your missionary. These can be had by writing to the missionary you support or to the board under which they serve. One of the best and most succinct was one which appeared in the Prayer Calendar of the United Methodist Church a number of years ago. It reads as follows:

How to Pray for Missionaries

Pray for essentials:

Health Enough To Glorify God.

> It is not so essential that you ask God to give us good health. The important thing is that He give us a measure of health that will glorify Him. We ought to be able to demonstrate to people about us that God can keep us in perfect peace and joy, even in the midst of pain.

Grace To Be Overcomers.

> We do not want you to pray that God will give us an easy path on our field of labor, but rather that He might give us grace sufficient to be overcomers for Him.

Time Enough To Pray.

> Pray not so much that God will answer our prayers, as that God will keep us from being too busy to pray. It is just as easy for missionaries as for anyone to be too busy to take time to be alone with God.

Determination To Go On.

> We are not so anxious for you to pray that God will remove obstacles as that He might give us an unconquerable determination to go all the way with Him.

God's Work To Do.

> It is not so important that you pray that God should bless our activities as that God would censor our activities. How easy it is for a missionary's time and energy to be spent on second-best things.

Strength To Resist Temptation.

> Please do not pray for us as though we were exalted saints living up on a high level just because we are missionaries. We who go as missionaries are subject to temptations. Satan will contrive in one way or another to hinder our testimony, to rob our lives of power or make our witness futile. We need your prayer that God will help us to resist temptation.

Patience, Joy, And Trust To Carry Us Through Each Day.

> Please remember that missionaries can become lonely, discouraged, irritable, sharp, and impatient with others. We can do a great deal of missionary work without being on fire. So we covet your prayers that we may live with hearts aflame with passion for the lost, aflame with the glory and love of God.

(used by permission)

There are many things you can do to develop a prayer ministry for missionaries. Following are several suggestions:

1. You might consider starting a Missionary Prayer Band where you pray for nothing or nobody but missionaries. Ideally, it ought to meet a least once a week. Certainly no less than once each month. You might consider meeting during a mealtime such as lunch and fasting during that meal. This could very well be a mission ministry to which God is calling you!

2. You might start a Prayer Partner Program where two or more covenant together to pray regularly for a missionary, perhaps at a given time each day.

3. Set as one of the goals of your Missions Conference a commitment on the part of your people to pray regularly for a missionary. They can sign a card for this just as they do for their Faith Promise.

For example, a little Church in Sandy Lake, Pennsylvania with only 285 members had a goal of 200 Prayer Partners and 238 actually signed up. Another church where the Faith Promise goal was $18,000 challenged their people to commit themselves to a, "Prayer Moment For Missions" and 83 people signed a card indicating that they would pray daily for a missionary. 83 x 365 = 30,295 prayer moments! Certainly that is more significant than any financial goal.

Some churches have little commitment cards which they sign and hang under the picture of a missionary on a Prayer Board. Duplicates of these cards are sent to the missionary so they can know who their Prayer Partners are and can, in turn, write and share their prayer needs thus making prayer more meaningful by making it more specific and personal.

4. List the names of your missionaries in the bulletin or church newsletter with their address and urge the members to write them telling them that they are praying for them. This will do two things. It will get the members to write the missionary and will lift the spirit of the missionary by knowing that someone is praying for them.

5. The Prayer Calendar published by the agency under which the missionary serves can be a valuable tool. Sometimes it is incorporated into their monthly newsletter or magazine and sometimes it is published as a separate item. Which ever is done, wide use should be made of the material they contain.

6. Make a list, on a little 3x5 card of the persons for whom you are praying and carry it in your pocket where it is easily accessible. Use it

during your devotions and at other times during the day. Sometimes I prop mine up on the dash of the car if I am driving any distance and glance at it from time to time. A friend of mine uses his as he drives to work and prays for missionaries when he has to stop for a red light. This sure beats fuming about the delay! Another friend says that he uses the list when he is caught in a line at the post office or a ticket counter.

7. When you are traveling long distances you can spend the time praying for missionaries. My wife and I take turns praying through the alphabet. She would try to think of a missionary whose name began with "A" and pray for them and I, in turn, would try to think of one whose name began with a "B". It is amazing how the miles roll by and the number of persons for whom you can pray.

8. Missionary names can be prominently displayed in the sanctuary on a hymn board or in the vestibule. The flag of the country in which they are serving can be displayed in the sanctuary, reminding people to pray, not only for the missionary but for the national workers and the people they are trying to reach.

As to ways to help remind people to pray for the missionaries, there is no want for ideas. All you have to do is let your mind be open to the Spirit. Remember that intercessory prayer is the most powerful force available to the child of God and through it we can make our influence felt anywhere in the world.

III. Praying for Unreached Peoples— Pray for the Harvest

You can't very well pray for harvesters and not pray for the people to whom you send them. We need to pray that ways may be discovered to reach them with the message of Christ's love, that their own culture may be the vehicle for the understanding of the gospel and that their hearts may be open and receptive to the Word.

In recent years, praying for unreached people has become an important prayer concern of the Church. Many organizations are helping to acquaint the church with the scope and nature of the Unfinished Task. The Church needs to learn to pray for a specific Unreached People Group. Just as it is important to pray for specifics for the missionary, so too, it is important to be specific when we pray for those who have not yet been reached for Christ. A number of helps are available.

1. *The Global Prayer Digest* published by the *U.S. Center for World Mission* is an excellent tool to help us become acquainted with,

and pray regularly for some of these groups. Every Christian would do well to acquaint himself with, and use, the Global Prayer Digest.

2. *The Mission Advanced Research and Communications* of Monrovia, California and *Operation Mobilization* of Waynesboro, Georgia both distribute packets of cards about Unreached People. These cards contain some basic information about the group; their geographic location, language, population and predominate religion together with some prayer needs. These are excellent to use each day since one can be slipped in a pocket or propped up on the desk or window ledge above the sink and can be glanced at from time to time. It is a great learning tool as well as a prayer reminder.

3. *Wycliffe Bible Translators* has an excellent program called *Bibleless Peoples Prayer Project.* They suggest that you recruit a prayer partner and together you covenant to pray for Unreached People. They will furnish you with basic information about the group and what their prayer needs are.

4. It is well, when possible, to have a large wall map so as to be able to pinpoint those areas where there are Unreached People. Wall maps can be secured from National Geographic, *The Naval Oceanographic Office* in Washington, DC or sometimes from your mission agency.

5. Flags can be made by the women of the church or secured from the United Nations. These can be used during your Missions Conference and then placed in the sanctuary from time to time and be used both as a teaching tool and as a prayer reminder for the people they represent.

******

In conclusion, and above all, it is well to remember that a great deal of effective mission work can be done without ever leaving home but on our knees before the Throne of Grace. We opened with a quote from Paul. We close with one. Romans 15:30, *I urge you...join me in my struggles by praying to God for me.*

Chapter 2

The Purpose of the Church

In this section we shall endeavor to point out that the business of the Church is worldwide witness. The task of the Work Area on Missions is to constantly remind the church of her purpose and to help her get on with the task.

It is of interest to note that Jesus never called His disciples to worship. They already were worshippers. He called them to witness. Unfortunately, the average Christian church seems to assume that when it has worshiped it has fulfilled its obligation as Christians. This may be why the organization, *Advancing Churches in Mission Commitment* tells us that only 2% of the 335,000 churches in America have a valid, ongoing missions program worthy of the name.

The Order Of Worship For The Reception of Members of the United Methodist Church says it well. It opens with the words, *The Church is of God and will be preserved until the end of time for the conduct of worship, the due administration of the Word and Sacraments, the maintenance of Christian fellowship and discipline, and the conversion of the world.* Certainly it is of more than passing interest to note that everything the Church does is bracketed by, *Worship...and the conversion of the world.* Worship and witness are the main purposes of the church. They are the two poles around which its whole world spins. Worship gives reason and empowerment for witness. Witness tells the world of Whom we worship and why we worship. It may very well be that worship that does not result in witness is not worship at all!

Ask any ten members of the church, "What is the purpose of the Church?" and you are likely to get essentially the same answer, "To tell the world about the love of God" or something similar to that. This is true whether they believe in missions or are opposed to them. This makes a good exercise, sometime, to open an Administrative Board meeting.

Our purpose for existence needs to be very clear. We do not exist merely for self-perpetuation, nor to provide a moral conscience for the community. The church is not merely a convenient means of marrying, burying and baptizing. We certainly are not a sort of religious fellowship where we enjoy the company of other like minded persons. It is not a place to which we come and doff our hats in God's direction. It may be all of these things, some of which are not bad. But, they are not the purpose of the church. Our purpose is worldwide witness. We are to reach every person possible, as quickly as possible with the Good News of the redeeming grace of God as revealed in Jesus Christ.

If we have no purpose we are like a satellite tumbling out of orbit. All that potential power going for naught. On the other hand, if we have a purpose it gives direction and meaning to everything the church does. Everything the church does should reflect and fulfill; that purpose. Everything the church does should be scrutinized and judged by that purpose. If it does not contribute to the fulfilling of that purpose it is not worthy of our time, money and effort and should be discontinued as quickly as possible.

The question is then, are we conscious of our purpose and are we consciously fulfilling it? The task of the Work Area on Missions of any church then, is unutterably simple. Our task is to constantly call the Church back to its primary purpose, namely the evangelization of the world until at last, *at the name of Jesus every knee should bow, in heaven and on earth and under the earth, and every tongue confess that Jesus Christ is Lord, to the glory of God the Father. (Philippians 2:10,11)* The task of the Work Area on Mission is to provide the church with the means to implement and fulfill its purpose. This makes the task of the Work Area on Missions the single most important task in the church!

Chapter 3

How to Introduce Missions to a Local Church

The purpose of this section is to give some suggestions and guidance for introducing missions to a church which has never had a strong mission program, or to a church which feels its mission responsibility is fulfilled when it pays its World Service apportionment. If a pastor has been appointed to a new church how does he or she go about introducing missions?

Imagine this scenario. You have been appointed to a new pastorate. You early discover, sometimes as early as the Pastor/Parish Relations Committee interview, that your new appointment has little or no mission vision beyond paying its World Service apportionment, and very often not even that! Or, you are a layperson and God has laid missions on your heart, yet you are a member of a church which, heretofore, has done little or nothing for missions. What do you do? How do you share your zeal for missions without alienating a lot of people?

First, you may take some comfort in the fact that you are not alone. You may be among the 98% of churches in America without a valid, ongoing mission program that occupies a place of priority in its planning. If misery loves company then you have a lot of company!

Secondly, you must also accept the fact that you are, in all likelihood, going to alienate some for there are always a few people who are going to remain hostile to missions even if St. Paul was appointed pastor of their church.

The average congregation (and where do you find an average congregation?) is usually composed of three groups. On the one hand, you have a small nucleus of dedicated persons who genuinely believe in missions and are just waiting for a pastor to give them some direction and encouragement. On the other hand, you have a small group of people, mentioned above, who are adamantly opposed to missions and are happy to tell you so every chance they get.

But, "in between, the misty flats, the rest (of the congregation) go to and fro." They are not opposed to missions, they just have not thought about it one way or another! They are going whatever direction the pastor is going. It is this group, perhaps representing a preponderance of the membership, that we must reach and to whom we must impart a vision for missions. How we accomplish this is the purpose of this chapter.

It is important that you avoid, at all costs, being negative or accusative. If a church is not enthusiastic about missions it may just be that they have never been challenged. Be positive. Proceed on the assumption that they are as committed to missions as you are, as though there isn't any question about whether we should do this. If we believe that missions, after worship, is the most important task of the church, then of course we will do it.

Very often pastors will want to wait until they get to know the congregation better before introducing something as controversial as missions are thought to be. Can you imagine waiting until you get to know the congregation better before having a worship service? Or we will want to wait until the mortgage is paid off or the church gets out of debt. That's getting the cart before the horse. I once was appointed to a church which had a huge mortgage and was deeply in debt for current expenses. They had not gone to conference with all apportionments paid within the memory span of the oldest members. We began to pray that God would help us to help them see beyond themselves. God answered my prayers through a natural catastrophe. The congregation rose to the occasion and responded beyond their wildest imagination.

During the first year or two of one's pastoral ministry the congregation is usually receptive to any suggestion from the pastor, believing the pastor has their best interest at heart. Take advantage of this honeymoon period to introduce missions. Begin to talk to a few key people. Ask questions. Find out what they have done in the past. Learn if the church has supported a missionary heretofore. Inquire if the church has produced any missionaries and if so, where are they now? Usually a church is proud of its past accomplishments.

Begin immediately to disseminate mission information through the church bulletin and newsletter. Insert the leaflet, **Church Around The World**, in the Sunday bulletin. Include a **Mission Minute** in the worship service. Start praying for missionaries by name during the morning worship service and all other meetings of the church. Urge your people to purchase copies of the **Prayer Calendar** published by the Board of Global Ministries. Use the **Guide to Daily Prayer** published monthly by Good News. Write The Mission Society for United Methodists and ask for a list of their missionaries and begin to pray for them. Ask the Mission Committee to subscribe to **World Pulse** published by Evangelical Missions Information Service, P.O. Box 794, Wheaton, Illinois 60189. Quote from Jim Reapsome's editorials in that periodical. Subscribe to **Mission Frontiers** published by the U.S. Center for World Mission, 1605 Elizabeth Street, Pasadena, California 91104.

If there is not a mission bulletin board in the church, ask the Mission Committee if they would be willing to sponsor one. Make sure it is visible and attractive. Call it to the attention of the congregation from time to time.

Very early in your ministry you ought to take time for a serious discussion in Board meeting as to what they, the Board members, consider to be **the business** of the church. This gives you an opportunity to raise the questions, "How are we getting on with the job?" and "What is our church's involvement in this task?" This can set the stage for introducing mission programs to the church. It is well, also, to raise the question as to what percentage of the church's budget is devoted to, "telling the world about the love of God." In this connection it is good to have them begin to think about some giving goals for missions.

Very early in your ministry, preferably during the first year, the church should be approached about having a Missions Conference. A good time to do this is during a planning retreat. The question might be raised as to what programs or methods are used to promote missions. If the answer is, "nothing" or is rather nebulous, you can suggest a Missions Conference. It is helpful to have a layperson, from another church which does have a Missions Conference, share what it has done for their church.

The Missions Conference and missions program of the church should stand alone financially. In a chapter entitled, **Faith Promise Giving** under section III Building A Faith Promise Budget we discuss ways to help underwrite a Missions Conference. It is difficult, but necessary, to help the Board understand that missions will never adversely affect the current expense budget of the church. On the contrary, its effect will be a healthy one. I believe it can be demonstrated that every church which begins to take the Great Commission seriously finds that every other aspect of the church's finances are enhanced. God honors those who honor Him.

If the church has a unified budget (and I know of nothing that can kill interest in missions quicker than a unified budget, for it depersonalizes everything) try to persuade them to set up a separate budget for missions. Assure them that in this way missions will never infringe on the current expense budget of the church.

In conclusion, be positive, be upbeat, and be loving. Don't be antagonistic or confrontational about missions. Remember that we are not in the business of alienating people but winning them to the cause of missions. Remember, also, you are not going to accomplish every-thing over night. Sometimes it is years before your suggestions and plans come to fruition. Make all of this a matter of intense prayer.

Chapter 4

Formulating a Mission Policy for the Local Church

The purpose of this section is to discuss the necessity for, and means of developing a mission policy for the local church. If every mission agency feels it is necessary to have a policy to justify its existence and clarify its objectives surely the same should be true for the local church which is, after all, the ultimate mission sending agency.

Once we have established and clarified the purpose of the Church, it is imperative that a policy be formulated to help fulfill its announced purpose. Policy is to Purpose what a string is to a bow. However strong the bow may be, the arrow will never reach its target without a string to send it on its way.

I. The Value of a Mission Policy is That it:

A. Gives a sense of direction to the entire mission program of the church.
B. Provides a strategy for reaching long term goals.
C. Provides a means by which the Mission Work Area finds guidance for decisions that it must make with regard to support for missionary personnel and projects.
D. Avoids the embarrassment of emotional requests on the part of interested church members who have friends or family members or pet projects they would like to have the church support.
E. Gives continuity to the mission program despite changes in leadership.

II. A Mission Policy Should Include:

A. A clear statement of the Biblical basis for missions.
B. A statement of the denominational involvement and commitment to missions. For United Methodists this can be taken from any current copy of the Discipline.
C. A strong statement of the local church's commitment to both of the above.
D. A statement of both long and short term goals.

E. Provision for the involvement of all levels of church life, chil-
    dren, youth, adults, men, women, shut-ins, leadership of the
    Sunday School and all other organizations connected with the
    church.
F. Guidelines for the recruitment and qualifications of missionary
    candidates.
    1. Personal relationship with Christ
    2. Working knowledge of the Bible.
    3. Commitment to the local church.
    4. Technical or theological training.
    5. Effectiveness as witnesses here and now.
    6. Present involvement in the mission program of the
        church.
    7. Lastly, but certainly not least, do they have a sense of
        humor?
G. The basis on which support will be decided.
    1. Theological commitment of the individual—do they truly
        believe that Christ and Christ alone is the only hope of
        the world?
    2. The agency under which they are to serve.
    3. Type of ministry in which they will be involved, i.e., agri-
        cultural, church planting, evangelism, educational, med-
        ical, etc.
    4. Area of the world and/or nature of the group being
        reached, i.e. Unreached People group or established
        work.
    5. Personal needs of the individual or family—medical,
        educational, housing, etc.
H. The financial policy of the church
    1. Possible sources of support for missionary personnel and
        programs. Family, friends, Faith Promise budget or regu-
        lar church budget.
    2. Levels of support. How high or low will a church go in
        its support of a particular missionary, project or pro-
        gram.
    3. Method for receiving, recording and distributing funds.
    4. Designation of funds by donor.
    5. A method for reporting to the missionary and congrega-
        tion.

III. Steps to Formulating a Mission Policy

A. First, have your Mission Commission, Committee, Task Force or Work Area Chairperson request permission from the Administrative Board or Ad-Council to develop a mission policy.

B. Secure materials that will be helpful. A good source of help is the Missions Policy handbook which can be secured from *Advancing Churches in Mission Commitment.* Another good source of help are mission policy statements that have been developed by other churches. Copies of such can be secured by calling or writing the author or The Mission Society for United Methodists.

C. Be sure to seek the input of other leaders in the church such as Finance, Education, Evangelism, Social Concerns. Contact Sunday school teachers and leaders of the youth.

D. Once you have hammered out a policy, distribute copies among various church leaders, including the pastors and staff, for their consideration, correction and suggestions.

E. Present the finalized draft to the Administrative Board for adoption so that it becomes an official document of the church. Once it has been approved make sure that it is distributed to every member of the congregation.

F. A Mission Policy should be as comprehensive as possible so that every area of concern is covered but should be geared to the size of the church. A short statement but well thought out can be as comprehensive as a long and detailed statement. There should be room for flexibility and change in the policy. The policy statement itself should provide for change. Make sure, however, that everyone is informed of any changes that are made.

Finally, and above all, USE THE POLICY, FOLLOW THE POLICY, ABIDE BY THE POLICY! It will make for real progress and avoid a great many headaches, heartaches and much misunderstanding.

Chapter 5
Goal Setting for the Local Church and the Individual

In this section we will consider the importance of goal setting and consider some goals to be set. In connection with this section it might be well to review the chapter on Missions Conferences.

Goals are important both for the local church and for the individual worshiper. Many of us go through life accomplishing little because we don't have the courage to set some goals for ourselves. The same thing is true of churches. We are afraid of goals lest we don't attain them and become discouraged. Better to set some goals and not attain them than to have no goal at all. The best way to hit nothing is to aim at nothing.

I. How to Set a Faith Promise Goal and Build a Missions Budget

(See Chapter 6 on Missions Conferences under "Goal Setting", third Paragraph [page 28])

It is well, several months in advance of the Missions Conference, to set a date for the discussion of the church's Mission Budget and Faith Promise Goal. Urge the entire congregation to make this a matter of prayer. Make it clear that any member of the church is invited to attend this budget building session for any input they may want to make.

Start by listing on a large blackboard, if possible, or have printed ahead of time a list of all persons and projects presently supported by the church, together with the amount sent them in the present year. Discuss each one, raising the question as to which should be continued and which dropped. There will be some normal attrition resulting from retirements, death, or termination of service. Those remaining should be discussed for increase or reduction of support.

Next, raise the question, "What do we think God would do through this church next year if we were open and obedient to Him?" You must believe that God can and does speak through the Body of Christ and then trust the decisions they make. Go around the room asking each person to state what or who the church should be supporting. Once they are finished making their suggestions, total them up and ask the question! "Does this truly represent what this church should be doing?"

One of the goals that a church ought to be setting is to reach the point where it is giving dollar for dollar. That is, for every dollar spent on local expenses a dollar should be given to make Christ known beyond the local parish. Many churches are going even beyond that.

Of course this cannot happen over night. It may require a long period of growth. I know one church which set for themselves the goal of reaching the 50/50 level over a ten year period. Perhaps a good place to start is to examine the total giving of the church and see what percentage is presently going to missions and benevolence and share that information with the congregation.

A first goal that churches often set is 10%. A good start! Next they may set a goal of giving 15 or 20%. I always wanted my churches to be giving as much to missions as they were paying for pastor support. In today's economy in the United Methodist Church that can be a sizable sum.

Another goal that a church might set is to totally support one missionary. And why not? We support one pastor and that is a ministry to us while a missionary is a ministry to others.

We might also want to consider supporting fewer missionaries in larger amounts of money. Sometimes a church, after several years of holding Missions Conferences, will have a long list of missionaries and projects they are supporting. Sometimes the amount of support is so small that it hardly covers the cost of the missionary's visit to the church.

Churches may support a missionary who comes to them in two different ways. A per mo/yr support may be pledged for the term of service. If the church chooses not to make a longer commitment, a one-time gift may be given. The missionary's expenses should always be covered.

In this process of reducing the number of missionaries supported it is not necessary to arbitrarily cut off anyone's support, especially if they are still on the field. But, by natural attrition the number of missionaries can be reduced. They may retire or they may not be returning to the field. I believe God wants to tell us *who and what* He would have us support just as He wants to tell us how much He wants us to give.

It is well, to have available for ready reference the Policy which the church has established for the selection of persons and projects to support. This avoids any hard feeling and misunderstanding.

II. Some Things to be Considered

A. Be Sure That All Areas Of The World Are Covered By Your Concern.

J. T. Seamands has said that Christians are the only ones with twenty/twenty vision. They see the need overseas but they see the need at home as well. Your Missions budget should reflect that. There ought to be projects and persons who are laboring for Christ in the local community, the district, conference, nationally and overseas. It is helpful to categorize your Faith Promise Goals as: Jerusalem, Judea, Samaria and the uttermost part of the world and so list them when you publish your missions budget.

B. Make Sure That A Variety Of Interests Are Covered.

Remember that your congregation has a variety of interests sometimes based on their own vocation or profession. Some are only interested in Evangelism and Church Planting, others are interested in Agricultural, or Medical, or Educational missions. Some are only interested in supporting missions at home. Don't fight with them or alienate them. Take them where they are and pray that their vision will broaden. Provide in your missions budget something that will appeal to every level of your congregation. Don't forget projects that will appeal to children and youth.

C. Submit The Budget To Your Administrative Board.

Make sure that it has the approval of the Administrative Board so that it becomes part of the official program of the church. Let nothing be done in a corner. Have it clearly understood that the Missions Budget will stand on its own feet and will not be dependent on the Current Expense Budget of the church. Also have it understood that the Missions Budget is not a case of robbing Peter to pay Paul.

D. Follow-up.

Make sure that the congregation is kept informed of what their Faith Promise money is doing. They ought to receive a monthly report of what has been received and how it was dispersed. Letters from missionaries can help to keep them informed as to what their money is accomplishing. It is also well to have a time of prayer in the worship service when those who have made Faith Promises are prayed for that they will be sensitive to the way God may be providing for their Faith Promise.

III. Personnel Goals

Jesus had a prayer request He made to His disciples, *Pray that the Lord of the harvest will send forth laborers into His harvest.* Regretfully, the average congregation seldom takes this very seriously.

The church should, in connection with its Missions Conference, set some personnel goals. This can consist of a challenge for full time, short term, or work team service. It could even include commitment to some kind of involvement in local mission projects.

IV. Other Goals for the Local Church

A. Developing A Prayer Ministry For Missionaries

Suppose when the challenge is made for Faith Promise giving that the church be challenged to pray once for each dollar of the Faith Promise goal. If they have a goal of $25,000, there should be 25,000 times during the year when they breathe the name of a missionary in prayer.

B. A Commitment To Pray For Unreached Peoples

Each congregation should consider adopting an Unreached People Group for which they will pray. Learn as much as you can about that group of people. Pray that God will raise up harvesters to send among them. Try to develop some liaison with them. U. S. Center for World Mission tells us that there are hundreds of Unreached People Groups. There are also 335,000 churches in America. Think what might happen if each church adopted one of those People Groups for whom to pray. Think of the potential power of prayer!

C. Total Support for One Missionary

The church should set as its goal the total support of at least one missionary in addition to whatever else they may be doing.

D. Work/Witness Teams

The church should strive to send out at least one Work/Witness Team each year. Perhaps it could alternate between youth and adults.

E. Letters to Missionaries

The church should strive to see that each missionary they support receives one letter each month from someone in the congregation. (These can be E-mailed for immediate responses.)

F. Local Involvement

The church should commit itself to involvement in local mission projects such as visitation evangelism, prison ministries, hospital and shut-in visitation, ministering to street people and operation of a food pantry.

V. Personal Goals

Not only should the church set goals for the corporate Body of Christ but individual members of the Body should be challenged to some personal goals. Those goals might consist of such things as:

A. Reading one book on missions each year.
B. Visit one shut-in each month.
C. Visit one unchurched family a year. Think what this would do for the church's evangelistic outreach. This is truly home missions!
D. Write one letter a year to a missionary.
E. Cultivate one member or family in the congregation not now interested in missions or who has expressed opposition to, or doubts about, the whole mission enterprise.
F. Invite some overseas student or "MK" * into your home for a weekend or at least for a meal.
G. Become involved in some local mission project on a volunteer basis.
H. Pray for God to raise up harvesters—even if it is your own children or grandchildren. Give God the best that you have—your family.
I. Pray regularly for at least one missionary by name. Learn all you can about their needs.
J. Offer yourself for some short term or work/witness project.
K. Prayerfully consider the possibility of full time service as a second career.

On the next page is a sample of a Personal Commitment sheet that can be placed in the bulletin. This, too, can be an act of worship as well as the Faith Promise.

* Missionary Kid

Commitment to Personal Involvement

By God's Grace I Will, During the Next 12 Months...

__ 1. Read a book on missions.

__ 2. Visit a shut-in once each month.

__ 3. Visit one unchurched family this year.

__ 4. Write a letter to a missionary.

__ 5. Cultivate some family of the congregation who has shown no interest in missions.

__ 6. Pray regularly for a missionary.

__ 7. Pray for God to raise up harvesters from our congregation.

__ 8. Get involved in some local mission project or ministry.

__ 9. Offer myself for short term missionary work or work crusade.

__10. Pray about the possibility of my becoming a career missionary.

Check one or more of the above and place on the Altar as your gift of love.

NAME: _____

DATE: _____

"...they gave themselves first to the Lord and by the will of God, to us...so we want you to excel also in this...undertaking."
                                        II Corinthians 8:5,7

The above can be printed on an 8½ x 5½ sheet and inserted in the bulletin and placed on the altar or in the offering plate.

Chapter 6
The Missions Conference

This chapter will deal with what the Missions Conference is, what it can do for the local church, what the church has a right to expect from the conference. Such matters as setting dates, developing a program and presenting the matter to the Administrative Board will be discussed. We will also give some possible program structures for conferences of varying duration.

Isn't it interesting that nearly everyone believes that the business of the church is to tell the world about the love of God and yet, so seldom we ask, "How are we getting on with the job?" or, "What is the involvement or contribution of our local church to this unfinished task?" or, "What is my personal involvement?" The Missions Conference is a time when we are given an opportunity to find some answers to these questions. But it is more. It is a time of rejoicing as the membership hears reports of what is being accomplished in the world as a result of its efforts. It is a time when we learn how the borders of the Kingdom are being extended as a result of our efforts. It is a time of commitment as we learn what remains to be done. It is a time of spiritual uplift. I can honestly say that the Missions Conference along with the Lay Witness Mission did much to raise the spiritual level of the congregations which I served.

What is the Missions Conference? It is a period of time set aside in the calendar of the church when that which we believe is, **"the business of the church"** is spotlighted for special emphasis. We do this with most other areas of the church and so we should for missions. Stewardship and Finance has its Every Member Campaign or something comparable. Christian Education has a special week in September very often ending with Rally Day. Evangelism, Family life, Christian Unity and many others have a special time of emphasis, why not missions?

The Missions Task Force, or Work Area, in conjunction with the Council on Ministries or Ad Council, having decided on a Missions Conference, should set a date well in advance. We suggest at least six months, preferably a year. This date should be cleared with the Administrative Board so that it becomes the official program of the church for that period. Nothing else should be going on during that time. All other programs should be postponed or integrated into the

Missions Conference. This way, everyone will understand that this is **the most important thing that is happening in the church at that time!** The moment that the Administrative Board approves the program and dates, announcement should be placed in the bulletin and in the next issue of the Church Newsletter so that no one can say that they were caught unawares.

One of the first questions that will come up is, "How long should it be?" It can be anywhere from one day to one month. Peoples' Church, Toronto, Canada at one time ran their conference for one month—not just four Sundays a month but something going on every day during that month. There does seem to be some relationship between length of time and effectiveness. The objective of the Missions Conference is the saturation of the entire congregation at every level; children, youth, adults, men and women, and shut-ins with the mission message. This cannot be done effectively in a short time. We recommend starting on a Sunday and ending on a Sunday. What takes place between Sundays may vary from church to church but it does seem wise to start on a high day and end on a high day.

Many churches opt for a weekend conference, especially if it is for a first time. Even in this case, we suggest that you try to have a kickoff speaker on the Sunday before, or have the pastor preach on missions the preceding Sunday.

Whatever length conference you decide on, the program should be structured so as to reach every segment of the congregation at least once. Plan programs specifically aimed to reach each group at their level of interest. (You can encourage the groups such as a S.S. Class, Women's or Men's groups, Youth, Children...to plan their own activity with a missionary or missions emphasis.)

The two major concerns are program and personnel. One reason to set your dates well in advance is to be able to recruit speakers. This is not easy. How many you will need will depend on the length of your conference. A weekend conference, ideally, should have at least three speakers: (1) someone to coordinate the conference and bring a Biblical motivation for missions. A mission minded pastor or mission executive can do this, especially if they have had experience conducting Missions Conferences in their own church. (2) There should be, if possible, at least one overseas missionary. (3) Also someone who is involved in national or conference missions. The overseas and national missionaries are there to tell about **who is doing what and where**. The

Coordinator or Bible teacher is there to tell **why**. A week long conference, obviously, will need more missionary speakers, perhaps five or
six—several for the first half of the week and several for the last half.

Speakers should be selected who are of interest to the congregation.
It may be someone whom they have been supporting or someone in
whose field or project they have an interest. Most churches know little
about where their money goes or even what the church is doing within
the confines of their own conference, to say nothing of overseas. One
of the primary purposes of the conference is to provide the congregation with basic information about missions.

It is also well to have someone whom the congregation might be
interested in supporting such as a missionary candidate. Have several
areas of the world represented as well as different types of ministries,
i.e. evangelism, church planting, medical, technical, agricultural, etc.

Make the selection of your speakers a matter of prayer. The wrong
kind of missionary can set your program back ten years! Make sure,
whatever their task on the field, that they are Biblically motivated to
make Christ known. They should have a greater motivation than
humanitarianism but should be genuinely concerned about the reconciliation of lost humanity to a loving heavenly Father.

Goal Setting

Having a Missions Conference and not setting some goals is like
preaching an evangelistic sermon and not giving an invitation. Can you
imagine Billy Graham sending the congregation home after his sermon
without urging them to do something about what he had been preaching? Unfortunately, that is what we very often do in our mission programs. After you have informed and inspired people you should have
the courage to challenge them to do something.

Goals should be more than monetary. It is well to set some personnel goals. If Jesus requested His disciples to pray for harvesters, you
ought to have some goals for your church to produce full-time workers
in the Lord's harvest field. Other goals could consist of such things as:

1. A prayer ministry for missionaries.
2. A commitment to writing letters to missionaries.
3. Little ministries to missionaries such as sending greet-
    ing cards on birthdays and anniversaries or subscribing
    to a magazine for them or securing parts for broken
    appliances.

4. Involvement in some local or conference mission program.
5. A commitment to pray for some Unreached People Group.

Of course a Faith Promise goal should be set and cleared with the Administrative Board. It should be understood that this is over and above all other budget items and conference apportionments and will not detract from the regular budget of the church. Many churches are reluctant to set a Faith Promise goal, fearful that the church will not respond. Nothing could be further from the truth! Most churches have just been waiting for someone to challenge them and will respond far beyond anyone's expectations. This is a case where Jesus' admonition to, "Ask largely that your joy may be full" should be taken literally!

Choosing a Theme

It is well to choose an overall theme for your conference. This gives you something to which everything can be tied, displays, brochures, music, decorations, etc. A few suggested themes to help you get started along this line are:

1. As The Father Has Sent Me So Send I You.
2. And You Shall Be My Witnesses...
3. Here I Am Lord, Send Me.
4. The World Is Our Parish.
5. Let Go! Help Go! Go!
6. His Last Command—Our First Concern.
7. Is It Nothing To You?
8. How Shall They Hear?
9. Feeding Many Hungers—Quenching Many Thirsts.
10. Finishing The Task.

There is virtually no limit to the possibilities of themes. This is a good thing in which to involve the youth. Let them be involved in coming up with a theme. Make it a contest in which everyone can be involved.

Some Program Suggestions
for the Missions Conference

I. A One Day Conference

A. Obviously this should be designated as Mission Emphasis Sunday.

B. It should be preceded by a Prayer Vigil starting Saturday night and running until Sunday morning. 6 p.m. Saturday to 6 a.m. Sunday.
C. A Men's breakfast could be scheduled for as early as 7 a.m. For this you should select your strongest speaker. Let him challenge the men for involvement in a mission work/witness project.
D. A missionary speaker in Sunday School. You might have the Sunday School classes go together in age groups, Children, Youth and Adults.
E. Morning worship with a mission speaker and the receiving of Faith Promises.
F. A Churchwide International Dinner following the morning worship service.
G. A Youth Rally in the afternoon or evening. This can be before or run concurrently with the evening service.
H. An evening service with a challenge for Christian service.
I. A time of fellowship with the missionaries to follow the evening service.

II. A Weekend Conference

A. This should start with a twelve hour prayer vigil 6 a.m. to 6 p.m. Friday.
B. An International dinner Friday evening with speaker or speakers to follow.
C. Saturday morning Men's Breakfast.
D. Saturday Noon Ladies Luncheon.
E. Saturday Afternoon Youth Rally or a Youth Rally could be held following the evening service. This could be a Pizza Bash. It should be very informal but the young people should be challenged for commitment to service.
F. Saturday evening service. This can be a forum type service where each of the missionaries are given five minutes and then the floor is opened for questions. Do not close with a Question and Answer period, however. Have someone give a brief Biblical challenge for missions.
G. Sunday
    1. Early Morning Prayer Time With the Pastor and Missionaries.
    2. Sunday School in age grouping—children, youth and adults—with a missionary speaker in each group.

3. Morning worship all the missionaries should be intro-
    duced and a challenge for Faith Promise Giving.
4. Evening Worship with a challenge to something more
    than money.
5. Fellowship time to follow.

III. An Eight Day Conference

A. A twenty-four hour prayer vigil should be scheduled starting at
    8 a.m. on Saturday and running until, 8 a.m. on Sunday. (See
    Chapter 8 entitled "Pray, Pray, Pray")
B. Saturday p.m. A Men and Missions Banquet. (See Chapter 17 on
    Men And The Mission Program Of The Church)
C. Sunday School. Again grouping according to ages with missionary
    speakers.
D. Morning Worship
    1. Introduce all the missionaries and give them a brief
        moment to bring greetings.
    2. Try to have your strongest speaker. This might be a mis-
        sionary but might be your mission coordinator.
    3. Remember that the morning worship is not the place for
        reporting or information sharing. It is worship and should
        have a Biblical message on reason for, purpose of and/or
        motivation for missions.
E. Sunday evening
    1. Youth Rally with one of the missionaries who relates well
        to youth.
    2. Regular evening service with perhaps two speakers, one
        to make a visual presentation and the second to bring a
        Biblical challenge.
F. Monday Through Friday
    1. Youth Breakfast each morning before school (See
        Chapter 16 on Youth)
    2. 10 a.m. Neighborhood conversation groups (See Chapter
        12 on Neighborhood Conversation Groups)
    3. Noon luncheon for missionaries and guests.
    4. It is well to have one luncheon during the week to which
        the clergy and spouses of the District, and missions chair-
        person are invited. Don't forget to invite the District
        Superintendent and Bishop (if he is near enough). This

very often sparks an interest and a number of other conferences get started. Sometimes a Round Robin conference develops from it.

5. Consider having one luncheon during the week to which
   pastors of other churches in the community are invited.
   Cost of the luncheons should be a part of your Missions
   Conference Budget or underwritten by interested laymen.
6. Neighborhood conversation groups in the afternoon.
7. Children's Meetings after school.
8. Evening Service with two speakers, one to bring a visual
   report and the other to bring a Biblical challenge for missions. It is possible to have two speakers and the service
   not run over an hour and fifteen minutes. **Each speaker
   must be warned to keep to his allotted time.** Each can
   have twenty minutes. A typical order of service for an
   evening with two speakers is:
   a. Opening hymn and/or theme chorus.
   b. Prayer
   c. Introduction of the speakers-keep it brief!
   d. Visual presentation-no slide presentation or video
      should be over twenty minutes!
   e. Question and answer period. Make sure the pas-
      tor or the coordinator fields and repeats the ques-
      tion so all will know what is being asked and
      answered.
   f. Have a chorus or hymn allowing the group to
      stand before the second speaker.
   g. Second speaker with Biblical message—not
      more than twenty minutes. Since the greatest
      need of most churches is motivation, and since
      adequate motivation for missions is only found
      in the Word of God, it might be well, in place of
      the morning neighborhood conversation group,
      to have a 10 a.m. Bible Study at the church, open
      to all. The mission coordinator, or Bible teacher
      for the week could bring a series of Bible studies
      on the Biblical mandate for missions. Or this
      could be the series used in the evening as the
      assignment for the second speaker.

h.   Have a musical night when one of your missionaries with a good voice and musical talent, someone like Keith and Charlotte Brown, put on a
program of hymns written by missionaries and
then tell the story of how the hymn came to be
written—hymns like, "Does Jesus Care."

i.   Have a skit night when missionaries put on a skit
of what it is like trying to adjust to life in a for-
eign culture and learning a strange language.
This can be both informative and humorous.

j.   Have a panel night when all the missionaries
participate, answering questions from the congregation. A church in Albany, Indiana had what
it called, "Missionary Squares" patterned after
Hollywood Squares. They sold tickets and
packed the church.

k.   Most missionaries have a sense of humor. It is a
must to survive on the field. Have a missionary
couple put on a skit opening a box or barrel of
clothes shipped from the States. This can be
hilarious. You can write the missionaries ahead
of time and ask them if they can or will do any
of the above.

l.   Close with prayers.

m.   Fellowship hour to follow.

G.   Saturday

A free day for the missionaries, pastor and congregation
to relax. It is a good time for the missionaries to sight see
or shop. After all, the missionary has to take things home
to his wife and children. Not that the missionary is there
as a tourist but wouldn't it be tragic to be in Niagara
Falls, NY and never see the Falls? I have been in an area
and never seen anything but the airport, the road from the
airport to the church and the inside of the church!

H.   Sunday

1.   Early morning prayer time for the speakers, pastors and
members of the congregation to pray for the services and
the response to what they have seen and heard all week.
A good time to pray about their Faith Promise.

2. Sunday School with missionaries speaking to the various age groups.
3. Morning Worship with a Biblical challenge for Faith Promise Giving.
   a. It is important that this service be tailored so as to allow enough time for the speaker and for the taking of the Faith Promises. (More about the Faith Promise in Chapter 11 dealing with Faith Promises.) Some things can be deleted for one Sunday. Such things as the Choral Responses, Prayer Requests, Apostle's creed, etc. Allow the speaker at least twenty minutes remembering that it usually takes at least ten minutes to take the Faith Promises. Taking the Faith Promises should be done by the pastor or the Missions Conference coordinator. The missionary should never be put in the embarrassing position of appearing to be raising money for himself. I have been in services where I was asked to preach a rousing missionary message and take the Faith Promises and it was already five minutes to twelve!
   b. If possible the Faith Promises should be totaled and the result given to the congregation. This can be done during the singing of the last hymn. This is the time for the Doxology!
I. Sunday Evening
   This service can be one of Triumph and Testimony. It should be a challenge for something more than the giving of money. (See Chapter 5 on Goal Setting) A challenge should be given for a commitment to full time, short term, part time and volunteer service.
J. Sing A Triumphant Song. The service should end on a note of triumph.

IV. Month Long Conferences

A. The month long conference can be a variation of any of the above.
B. It can be four Sundays following the pattern of the one day conference.

C. It can be four weekends following the pattern of the three day con-
    ference.
D. It can be that all regular meetings of the church such as Ad
    Council, Prayer meeting, Men's, Ladies, Youth, and Choir could
    have a missionary speaker at their regular meeting.

**ONE FINAL WORD. BATHE EVERYTHING YOU DO IN
PRAYER. MAKE EVERY DECISION A MATTER OF PRAYER.
(See Chapter 8, "Pray, Pray, Pray!")**

Our Vigil of Prayer

(To be used as an example of prayer)

THINK OF OUR LORD SPEAKING TO YOU, AND SAYING,

"My child, I am glad that you have come here to this quiet place at this time to fellowship with Me in prayer. All through this busy week of meetings here at the church, in addition to your hectic activities of daily living, I have been longing to meet with you in a deeper, more intimate way. I have been wanting you to really share the burden that sent Me to Calvary for you, and for the sins of all mankind. I have been wanting you to get a fresh and renewed vision of the lostness of humanity and the reality of My love for them. I have been working in your heart so that you might love me more, in order that you might have a much greater concern for bringing a lost world to Me than you have ever had before. Put out of your mind just now anything concerning your personal selfishness or desires that might stand in the way of our fellowship together. Tonight, for these brief moments, let your prayers concentrate on the needs of others, and I will show you what you can do to help Me reach them." Read II Cor. 8:9.

"First, I have given you the wonderful privilege of living in a land where My Word is known and loved and preached. Have you some thoughts of praise or thanks for this? Without it, you know this moment would not be happening!" Read Psalm 34.

"Secondly, my child, let Me take the burden of the sins and the cares that have been oppressing you and disturbing the perfection of our relationship. Confess them to Me now, that I might bear them for you. If you regard iniquity in your heart, you know, it will mar our communion, and I cannot really hear you as you pray," Now read Psalm 66:18, I John 1:9 and I John 2:1,2.

"Now I would like you to think of My servants who are faithfully witnessing for Me throughout the world tonight. Think of the part that your church has been taking in making their witness possible. Do you realize that without you their work could not be done? I have made you and all men in such a way that none of you can live unto yourself; you are dependent one upon another. Are you thankful for them? Are you glad for your part in their work? They are my servants, you know, and it is My will that you pray for them without ceasing, and share in their temporal needs as well..." Read Ephesians 6:19, II Cor. 1:11. I Cor. 9:14.

"I long for you to be really concerned about the great lack of laborers in the harvest. Do you not see it? I am not willing that any should perish, but oh, the laborers are so very, very few! Why don't you pray that many of your youth will hear My voice and offer their lives for My work? Are you afraid to do this? Are you afraid that it might be your own children that I need? Can't you trust Me with their lives while they are away from you? And what about some of your young married couples and even older folk who have talents and skills that I would like to use elsewhere in the world; can you pray that these too, will hear My voice? And how about you? I have a very special plan for you alone. I want your own life totally committed to Me so that I can use you where I need you. Will you let Me have it?" Read Luke 10:2, Romans 12:1-2, Isaiah 6:8-9.

"And now, my child, I would like to tell you what your part in this great outreach is to be. Does our 'Faith Promise' goal stagger you? I can do this and even much more, if you'll trust Me! Will you just open your heart to My voice, and quietly listen? I have blessed you far beyond the average of your fellow men throughout the world. Now I would like to have you reach out in faith and covenant with Me to return a portion of that which I am going to place in your hand throughout this coming year. Trust Me! I will not fail you. Step out in faith, and you will find a greater blessing in store for you than you ever have known before!" Read II Cor. 9:6-8, Phil. 4:15-19, and John 16:23.

LET'S TRUST THE LORD FOR A GREAT VICTORY!

Prepared by the Rev. Donald T. McIntosh

Chapter 7
How to Reach Your Own People

The purpose of this chapter is to help the Missions Committee reach the members of the congregation with the mission message and persuade them to attend the meetings of the Missions Conference.

For the Missions Committee, their task is not over after they have set a date for the Missions Conference, set a Faith Promise budget, secured the speakers and planned the program. In fact, the hardest part of their task is just beginning and that is devising ways to get their own people out to the meetings.

I. What Makes it Difficult?

It is a well known fact that, of all the activities in which the church engages, missions has the lowest level of interest on the part of the congregation. Nothing the church does receives as little attention as a mission program. People stay away from missions meetings in great numbers. This is so for a number of reasons. First, we live in an entertainment oriented society and people expect to be entertained, even when they come to church and missions is usually not entertaining even though most missionaries have a keen sense of humor or they would never have survived on the mission field. Or, the congregation may have had a bad experience with a missionary who showed a poor set of slides and droned on and on about people in the pictures.

Another reason for the low level of interest in missions is that we suspect that we are going to be challenged to do something and we just don't like to be challenged.

But, perhaps, the main reason for lack of interest in missions is that a high percentage of the congregation has never been convinced that worldwide witness is the business of the Church. For some odd reason our worship has not led to witness. Therefore, the task of the mission committee is an unenviable one. Not insurmountable, but not easy.

II. Why Did it Only Happen Once?

There is an interesting line in Acts 21:18. Paul and his travelling companions had arrived in Jerusalem from what is referred to as Paul's third missionary journey. They are reporting their activities to James and the Church in Jerusalem and it says, "and all the elders were present." That is probably the last time that could be said in the history of the Church! But, they had an "edge of their seats" interest in what God was doing through Paul's ministry to the Gentiles.

III. How Do You Get Your Own People Out?

If we believe that one of the purposes of the Missions Conference is the total saturation of every level of the congregation with the mission message and challenge, then it is the task of the missions committee to devise means by which everyone in the congregation is reached. (See Chapter 6 entitled The Missions Conference)

How do you get your own people to attend the meetings of the Missions Conference? Ah, that is the question. First, you start with the committee members themselves. They must be committed to what is going on. They have known for months the dates for the conference and should have been able to clear their calendar so that nothing short of personal illness or death in the family should keep them away!

Next, if every member of the missions committee were to adopt one family of the congregation which had shown little or no interest in missions and invite them to their home for dinner or to the international dinner held in connection with most Missions Conferences, telling them they did not have to bring a thing, even offering to pick them up, that would at least guarantee that the attendance would be double the number on the missions committee!

Every member of the committee knows other members of the congregation that have shown a genuine interest in missions. Get them to invite others to accompany them to the meetings. Such people can become your best publicity agents.

IV. Don't Be Afraid to Be Commercial

Be willing to sell tickets to some events such as the ladies luncheon or tea and the men's banquet or breakfast. Strangely enough, some people feel an event is more significant if they have to pay for it. Young people make good ticket salespersons. I was in a Missions Conference where the youth sold tickets for the missions banquet and were allowed to keep 50¢ of every ticket sold for their own missions program. (See Chapter 17 on Men And The Mission Program of the Church)

V. Use the Missionaries and Missionary Children

Perhaps you could have one night when the missionaries put on a talent show and tickets could be sold for that. Many missionaries have a wealth of talent to share. Often, on the field they must provide their own entertainment.

If the missionaries have brought their children with them, which is often the case, have the children share what life is like in a different culture. This can be both educational and entertaining.

VI. Use the Youth

We were in a Missions Conference where the youth of the church represented the missionaries whom the church supported but who were not there. They acted in first person, telling where they served, what the country was like and what they did. It was a fun time for the congregation and educational for the young people.

VII. Use Your Shut-ins

Your shut-ins, even though they cannot get out to the meetings can call every family of the congregation and urge them to attend the meetings. They can also pray for the meetings. (See Chapter 19 entitled, "Don't Forget the Shut-ins")

VIII. Make Attendance a Matter of Prayer

Just as you pray for unreached people groups so pray for unresponsive church members. Adopt a family and pray for them that they will become as enthusiastic about missions as you are.

IX. Some Things Not to Do

Above all, don't depend on the church newsletter or bulletin or even an announcement from the pulpit, by the pastor, to get the people out to the meetings. That can be deadly! People seem to pay little attention to announcements in the bulletin and not much more attention to an announcement by the pastor than they do to his or her sermons!

Invitation to missions meetings must be done on a one-to-one basis. Nothing beats a personal invitation. After all, that is how many of us came to Christ.

Chapter 8

Pray, Pray, Pray!!!

This chapter will deal with the importance of seeking God's guidance and blessing on every decision that is made, every program that is planned, every speaker who is invited, on everything that is done in connection with the Missions Conference. A Prayer Ministry for Missionaries will be discussed in a later chapter.

We cannot stress too strongly the place and importance of prayer in preparation for and during the Missions Conference. If I were asked to name the five things that would assure you of a successful conference they would be:

> **PRAYER**: Make everything a matter of prayer. Pray about dates, program, speakers, length of time, goals—everything!

> **PERSONNEL**: Personnel are critical. Make the selection and securing of your speakers a matter of prayer.

> **PRAYER**: Put prayer at the center of everything you do!

> **PROGRAM**: Pray about the type of program, time, schedule, length, etc.

> **PRAYER**: After you have done everything, humanly, that you can do, resign the whole thing to God. It is really His program!

It is advisable to select persons for the Missions Committee who are known to be persons of prayer. They should be urged to make the missions program of the local church a matter of regular, daily prayer. Since missions is, very often, a controversial matter in many churches or is a matter of indifference on the part of many members it is vital that nothing be done without prayer.

Urge the committee members to pray about dates, selection of speakers, structuring of the program and the presentation of the Missions Conference to the Administrative Board.

Once decisions have been made about the dates, program and personnel, begin to pray about the matter of setting goals; financial and otherwise. Invite the entire congregation to join in prayer about these matters. This does several things. It gets the membership thinking about the Conference and makes them feel that they are important and can have a vital role in the planning.

All groups of the church, (Sunday School Classes, Bible Study groups, Prayer groups) should be asked to pray for the Missions Conference. At least once each month there should be special prayer during the morning worship service. If the pastor has a silent prayer time in the service, request that those connected with the Missions Conference be prayed for. If prayer requests are asked for, mention the Missions Conference. Try to be specific. Ask different groups to pray for one of the leaders or speakers.

Sometime prior to the start of the Missions Conference a Twenty Four Hour Prayer Vigil should be held. A good time for this is the 24 hour period just ahead of the starting service. A chart showing 48 half hour segments can be placed in the Narthex or on the bulletin board. Sign-up sheets can be passed throughout the congregation during the morning worship service, giving people an opportunity to sign up. They can sign as individuals or as families. Once the sign up sheets have been correlated it may be necessary to ask some to shift their half hour so that all slots are filled. One good procedure is to ask the women to come to the church during the 8 a.m. to 4 p.m. period, the youth to be responsible for the period 4 p.m. until midnight and the men to be responsible for the eight hour period from midnight until 8 a.m. Youth very often respond very well to this kind of challenge. Having each group assume responsibility for an eight hour segment does not mean that they cannot come at other times if it is more convenient. Often we would see whole families in the sanctuary during the wee hours of the morning.

It is well to provide some Prayer Vigil guidance sheets, giving them some scripture passages to read, perhaps some instances of answered prayer during previous Missions Conferences, some guidance as to what to pray for and the list of speakers who will be coming to the conference. (See pages 35-36 *Our Vigil of Prayer*)

Don't forget your shut-ins. This is one good way to involve them in the Missions Conference. Write them a letter urging them to pray for the conference. Tell them that they, too, can sign up for one of the prayer vigil periods even thought they cannot come to the church during that time. Let the others know that the shut-ins will be praying also.

Before or after each of the services it is well to gather the speakers, committee members, pastors and any others who might be interested to join in a prayer time. If we can have a social hour following the services we should also be able to have a prayer time. It is especially important that Saturday evening, following the service, time be spent in prayer for the Sunday services. Pray for those who will be leading the service, the pastor, the organist and song leader or choir director, the ushers, the choir, the special music, the speaker that he may have a fresh message from the Lord. Pray also for that whole host of people who will be coming to the worship service and may not have been to a single event during the Missions Conference. They may come expecting to hear their beloved pastor preach and then be disappointed that a stranger, especially a missionary, is speaking. Remember, it is our desire to win people, not to alienate them.

Pray for whoever is to lead the Faith Promise portion of the service. This takes real skill and finesse. Unfortunately, the taking of the Faith Promises usually comes at the close of the service and means that the service may run longer than usual. It takes ability and inspiration to do the job effectively and keep the congregation in a good humor, especially when the service is running overtime.

If there is an evening service during which time there will be a call for commitment to Christian service or some kind of mission involvement, make this also a matter of prayer, that God will speak to hearts and they will respond to His call.

Chapter 9
Missions Conference Committees

Following are some suggested committees for the Missions Conference. Each local church may find it necessary to structure the committees according to local needs and available personnel. Smaller churches may want to combine committees. It is wise to involve as many persons as possible in committee work. Ask committee chairpersons to recruit at least five people to assist them.

You can recruit for committees, conversation group hostesses, housing and feeding of missionaries by inserting a check sheet in the Worship Service bulletin and church newsletter several weeks in advance of the conference and inviting people to check the things they are willing to do. Make it part of their offering. Involve everyone you can! (See Chapter 10, "How to Secure Volunteer Help")

It is good to have a recognition-dedication service just before the Missions Conference where appreciation can be expressed to those who have worked to make the conference a success.

Prayer Committee

Purpose - To mobilize the entire church into a mighty prayer movement for the conference. If we were to single out any one committee as the most important, it would have to be the Prayer Committee.
Duties
1. The moment the date is set, ask the pastor to include prayer for the conference in the worship services.
2. Contact every class and organization of the church, urging them to make prayer for the conference part of every meeting.
3. Arrange for neighborhood prayer groups.
4. Plan a prayer vigil prior to the conference.
5. Give guidance on what to pray for: The Faith Promise goal, personal involvement and commitment; personal response; for God to send forth laborers into the harvest; and for the speakers who will be participating.

Program Committee

<u>Purpose</u> - To Plan activities that will reach every segment of the congregation as often as possible during the Missions Conference.
<u>Duties</u>
1. Secure speakers, workers, song leaders as early as possible. One year in advance is not too soon.
2. Consult with youth leaders, Sunday School officials, men and women's groups, and all other organizations such as Scouts, to coordinate their programs with the conference.
3. Schedule meetings so that the largest number of people can attend as many meetings as possible. Make the wisest use of time. Have no dead spots.
4. Be imaginative. Plan all sorts of meetings, Youth breakfasts or pizza party, children's meetings, men's banquets or breakfasts, Ladies luncheons, rallies, cantatas, etc.

Publicity Committee

<u>Purpose</u> - To make sure the membership and community are aware of the time, nature and purpose of the conference.
<u>Duties</u>
1. The moment the Administrative Board approves the dates, get it into the church newsletter and bulletin.
2. Secure biographical sketch and glossy print of the speakers.
3. Prepare a promotional leaflet.
4. Arrange for media coverage.
5. Plan for some type of sign or banner outside the church.

Finance Committee

<u>Purpose</u> - To estimate all expenses of the conference and plan for income to cover them.
<u>Duties</u>
1. Prepare a budget for the conference
2. Devise a plan for meeting expenses through offerings, or as part of the Faith Promise Budget.
3. Provide for receiving and recording all offerings during the conference.
4. Pay all bills, including the travel and honorarium for speakers.

5. Be prepared to total Faith Promises on the closing Sunday. Provide for a method to record and distribute all moneys received through the Faith Promises. Be sure to inform the congregation of how they can participate in Faith Promise giving.
6. Keep the congregation informed as to where their money went and what it is accomplishing.

Hospitality and Transportation Committee

<u>Purpose</u> - To care for the needs of speakers. (See Chapter 21 entitled "The Care & Feeding of Missionaries.")
<u>Duties</u>
1. Secure housing for speakers. Inquire of them as to their needs and preference. Be sure to invite their spouses!
2. Arrange for meals. Inquire about dietary needs.
3. Check with speakers as to mode of travel and time of arrival. Arrange for someone to meet them at the airport or bus terminal. Make sure that someone is there when they arrive!
4. If it is a Round-Robin conference or a District affair, arrange for transportation between churches.

Attendance Committee

<u>Purpose</u> - To insure a good attendance at all meetings. Without doubt, after the Prayer committee, this is one of the most important groups.
<u>Duties</u>
1. Have a lay person speak to all groups in the church, urging their support and attendance.
2. Use the fill-a-pew plan.
3. Urge classes and groups to attend in a body or incorporate their regular meeting into the conference.
4. Use the telephone. Involve shut-ins as a telephone team to call the entire membership of the church.
5. Urge youth and adults to look on the conference as an evangelistic opportunity to win people to Christ.
6. Urge every member of every committee to be responsible for bringing someone to at least one of the services; persons who might not otherwise come to anything.

Music Committee

<u>Purpose</u> - To confirm and support the missionary message through music.

<u>Duties</u>
1. Secure a song leader and/or soloist for the conference.
2. Involve the church choirs-perhaps presenting a missionary cantata.
3. Choose a song or chorus that fits the theme of the conference.
4. Arrange for a pianist or organist for every service.
5. Arrange for special music for each service. Schedule it well in advance.

Urge those who are providing special music to keep it in harmony with the meeting. Use no one who will not stay for the entire service. Music is a support to the service, not a display of talent.

Displays Committee

<u>Purpose</u> - Provide for a literature table for visiting missionaries and display of curios.

<u>Duties</u>
1. Select a site near the center of activities during the conference.
2. Provide tables for displays and literature.
3. Provide help, if needed, for the missionaries to set up their displays. Provide for a display of good missionary books.

Food Services Committee

<u>Purpose</u> - To arrange for all meetings involving meals and refreshments.

<u>Duties</u>
1. To arrange for food to be provided for all banquets, breakfasts and luncheons.
2. To secure groups or individuals to provide refreshments following evening services.
3. To arrange for a treat at the children's meetings.
4. Arrange for the cost of all meals and refreshments to be amply met either by inclusion in the Missions Conference budget, by sale of tickets, or by free will offerings.
5. Arrange for cleanup of dining hall or social area and kitchen after all meetings.

Posters and Banners Committee

<u>Purpose</u> - To stimulate interest in the conference. Provide information about missions. This committee should work closely with the Publicity Committee. In fact, could be a subcommittee of it.
<u>Duties</u>
1. Prepare a large banner for the sanctuary with the theme of the conference.
2. Encourage children and youth to make banners and posters on mission themes.
3. Arrange for an award for the best poster or banner by each age group. Presentation of the awards could be made a part of one of the services.
4. Arrange for posters to be displayed in prominent places around the church, well in advance of the conference.

Audio Visuals Committee

<u>Purpose</u> - To assist in getting the missions message across through audiovisuals.
<u>Duties</u>
1. Contact speakers in advance, advising them of the number of slide presentations or videos they will be expected, or have opportunity, to make.
2. Advise missionaries as to exactly how much time they have to make their presentation and let them know that you expect them to adhere to it!
3. Provide necessary equipment and make sure it is in good working condition. Have extra bulbs and extension cords available.
4. Give the missionaries whatever assistance they may need in getting set up.

Nursery (Baby Sitters) Committee

<u>Purpose</u> - To make it possible for the parents of small children to attend the services. See if you can secure the services of a sister church to provide baby sitters so no one of the congregation will have to miss meetings.
<u>Duties</u>
1. Arrange for nursery attendants, making sure there is always a responsible adult in charge. *Youth may be used only as assistants.*

2. Let attendants know the times they will be needed. Check with them to make sure they know when they are to be on duty. Leave nothing to chance.
3. Make sure nursery is lighted, heated and clean.
4. Provide whatever materials may be needed by the attendants.
5. Inform parents through the bulletin, newsletter and publicity leaflet that a nursery will be provided.

Ushers Committee

Purpose - To see to the care and handling of the crowds (hopefully!) that will be attending the meetings.
Duties
1. Meet with the ushers and usher captains and inform them of the meetings for which they will be responsible.
2. Have ushers be prepared to receive the offering at each service, if one is taken.
3. Give the ushers guidance as to how and when to distribute and collect the Faith Promise cards.
4. It is well, if possible, to have an usher or two at all meetings such as luncheons, breakfasts, etc. They usually know where the light switches and heat and air conditioning thermostats are and are prepared to handle emergencies.

Chapter 10

How to Secure Volunteer Help for a Missions Conference

One of the reasons for reluctance to conduct a Missions Conference is the fear that there will not be enough help to pull it off. This is almost never true. The average church has more people willing to help than it ever uses. It is said that 80% of the work in the church is done by 20% of the people. Part of the reason for this is that the other 80% are never asked. We have a way of asking people we feel will say, "Yes." Consequently, we use the same people over and over until they experience burnout. Some people are never asked because it is feared, or felt that they will say, "No" so why bother asking them.

Most people are honored that they are asked even when they have a legitimate reason for refusing. But, don't ever answer for anyone! Give them the privilege of saying yes or no. Don't become discouraged by the first refusal. Tell them you will be back again to ask them to take on another task.

How to secure volunteers so that a large number of the congregation is involved? First, urge committee chairpersons and members each to recruit three or four persons to help them with their task. Everyone in the church has several friends that they feel free to call on for help. This does several things. It helps the committee members to know they do not have to do it alone; It also broadens the base of support for the mission program. Sometimes persons who may not even believe in missions will become involved because a friend asked them to do something.

Secondly, about a month before the conference, enclose in the bulletin a check list of things for which you will need volunteers for the Missions Conference. (See sample on page 53.)

Take a few moments in the worship service to explain the check list and give your people a few moments to look it over, pray about it and fill it out. Then, have them place them on the offering plate as part of their offering that morning. Unfortunately, people seldom think of volunteer service as an act of worship but the giving of my time and talent, or using my automobile, or sharing my home can be as much an act of worship as the giving of my money. The check list might be placed in the bulletin on successive Sundays.

We were always surprised at the persons who would volunteer to do things. Persons it would never occur to us to ask. Especially things like housing or providing meals. There are persons who are good hosts and very hospitable but are not enthusiastic about missions. Sometimes having a missionary stay in their home is the best way to promote missions.

Check List for Volunteers for Annual Missions Conference

at _____(Name of Church) _____(Dates)

Our Goal: Everyone Doing Something!

___ 1. Provide housing for a missionary. "Prepare a guest room for me..." Philemon verse 22

___ 2. Provide a meal for a missionary. "I was hungry and you gave me food." Matthew 25:35

___ 3. Provide transportation for children's meetings, youth breakfasts or for the missionary. "I hope...to have you assist me on my journey." Romans 15:24

___ 4. Help with youth breakfasts. "Jesus said to them, 'Come and have breakfast' " John 21:12

___ 5. Help with Youth Pizza Bash. "When He was at the table with them He took bread...then their eyes were opened and they recognized Him." Luke 24:30,31

___ 6. Help with Children's Meetings. "Let the little children come to me." Mark 10:14

___ 7. Act as Host and Hostess at the International Dinner. "Blessed are those who are invited to the Marriage Supper of the Lamb." Rev. 19:9

___ 8. Help with the Men's Mission Banquet. "All ate and had their fill...and those who ate were about 5000 men." Matthew 21:14,15

___ 9. Help with decorations—flags, displays, etc. "His Banner over me is love." Song of Solomon 2:4

___ 10. Clean Up Committee. "Select...seven men...whom we may appoint to this task." Acts 6:3

___ 11. Baby Sit. "People were bringing little children to Him...and He took them up in His arms...and blessed them." Mark 10:1,2

___ 12. Host Neighborhood Conversation Groups. "He was home...many gathered around...and He was speaking words to them." Mark 2:1,2

___ 13. Help With Publicity. "...the woman went back into the city. She said to the people...come see a man..." John 4:28,29

___ 14. Telephone Committee. "I called him but he did not answer." Song of Solomon 5:6

___ 15. Help with Book Table. "...and the books were opened..." Revelation 20:12

___ 16. Photographic Record of the Conference. "...It was I who multiplied visions..." Hosea 12:10

___ 17. Other. Please Specify _____
"Now Jesus did many other signs in the presence of His Disciples." John 20:30

Name _____

Address_____

Phone Number _____

Signed _____
(please fold and place in the offering plate)
(This check sheet can be printed on two sides of an 8½ x 5½ sheet for easy insertion in the bulletin.)

Chapter 11
Faith Promise Giving

In this section we will discuss the whole scope of Faith Promise giving; what it is not, what it is, how to build a Faith Promise budget, how to take the Faith Promise, sources of Faith Promise money, reporting and follow up. We will also share testimonies of churches and individuals.

I. What the Faith Promise is Not

It is not a stewardship gimmick. It is not a new and fancy term for pledging. Pledging is predicated on present possessions or anticipated income, Faith Promise is not. It is not a part of our tithe. It is not a case of shifting our present giving, that is, moving money from one pocket to another. It is not a case of robbing Peter to pay Paul.

II. What it is

A Faith Promise is the result of seeking God's will for your financial commitment to missions. It is a case of entering into a covenant with God that, as He provides, you will give. While a pledge is predicated on present possessions or anticipated income, a Faith Promise is predicated on the inexhaustible riches of Almighty God, who owns the cattle on a thousand hills, the wealth in every mine, and His willingness to channel them through you for the blessing of His world.

Someone has called the Faith Promise, "giving what we cannot see or do not have", based on the familiar Scripture in Hebrews 11:1 that "faith is the substance of things hoped for, the evidence of things not seen." Vince Rutherford, long time missionary under the Board of Global Ministries of the United Methodist Church, has a definition of Faith Promise giving that I like. He says, "Faith Promise giving is designed for those who don't have what they would like to give but are willing to be channels through which God can give."

Whatever else, Faith Promise giving, like all other things God asks of us, is intended for our blessing. It is not for His benefit for He has need of nothing that we have, but it is for our blessing. It is a blessing to enter into a covenant relationship with God, knowing that you can trust Him to be faithful to His Word and that He can trust you to be faithful to your promise. It is a blessing to watch God work and do that which seems to us to be impossible.

In Faith Promise giving two basic Christian principles come into focus—Faith and Obedience. We must have faith to believe that God is willing to tell us how much He wants to give through us, just as we believe that He wants to direct all other areas of our lives. We must then obey whatever it is He tells us, however ridiculous it may seem to us to be. God seems to be in the habit of issuing commands which appear to be, based on human logic and reason, utterly ridiculous. Our obedience then becomes an act of Faith—perhaps the highest form of faith—trusting Him when we cannot anticipate how He will provide. Faith Promise giving is a tangible expression of the great triumvirate—Believe, Obey, Trust.

In the last analysis, Faith Promise giving is a blessing because it is Biblical. In the story of the Good Samaritan in Luke Chapter 10, we are told that, "the next day when he got ready to depart he took out two silver coins and gave them to the innkeeper and said, 'Take care of him.' (That was a cash contribution) But, the Samaritan went on to say, 'And whatever extra expense you incur, I will reimburse you when I return.' " **(That was a Faith Promise!)** It was tantamount to giving the innkeeper a blank check. In Faith Promise giving you allow God to determine the amount!

In II Corinthians 8:1-3, Paul writes, *And now brothers, we want you to know about the grace that God has given to the Macedonian church. Out of their most severe trial, their overflowing joy and their extreme poverty, welled up in rich generosity. For I testify that they gave as much as they were able...(that was a pledge), but even beyond their ability. (That was a Faith Promise!)*

Note that neither Jesus nor Paul criticizes the Samaritan or the Macedonian church for financial irresponsibility. They are not cautioned against foolish financial commitments. Instead they are commended for their action.

If you want to know the real joy of Christian giving, I urge you to try Faith Promise giving.

III. Building a Faith Promise Budget

First, we must believe that God does speak through the Body, revealing His will for a local congregation. Set a date for the building of the Faith Promise Budget. This should be at least three months in advance of the Missions Conference. Any interested member of the congregation should be invited to attend for their input. Thus, the Faith

Promise Budget becomes more than something handed down by the Conference or dreamed up by the pastor or a select group in the church. Having been created by the members of the congregation it is much more apt to be supported by the entire congregation.

A. What It Should Cover.
1. Recognizing that God has raised up many different ministries for the blessing of His world and that the congregation has a variety of interests, the Faith Promise Budget should represent a wide range of ministries.
2. Some churches break their Faith Promise budget down into the following:
   a. Jerusalem (local mission projects)
   b. Judea (conference projects)
   c. Samaria (national projects)
   d. Uttermost Parts Of The World (overseas missions)
3. It should include support for individual missionaries, projects, and a variety of ministries such as medical, educational, agricultural and technical.
4. There ought to be an item to help make it possible to send youth and adults on mission work/witness teams. This can be done by offering to pay half the cost if the individual will pray about and ask God to provide the other half. Sometimes the way God works to provide money is as great a blessing as the trip itself.
5. Another item that might be included is scholarship money for an overseas student.
6. Be sure to include in the Faith Promise budget an amount for mission promotion. This is the way to finance your next Missions Conference. The mission program of the church ought to stand on its own and not be dependent on the Current Expense Budget of the church.
   If a church is holding its first Missions Conference and there is no money appropriated for it there are a couple of ways it can be underwritten.
   a. The pastor might designate money that comes to him from funerals, baptisms, or special speaking engagements.
   b. A few lay persons who are known to have an interest in missions might be approached and asked if

　　　　they might be willing to make a contribution to get
　　　　it started.

7.　One of the reasons for an item in the Faith Promise
　　　Budget entitled, "Mission Promotion" is so that missions
　　　can be promoted all year.

8.　Also, if you happen to have a mission speaker during the
　　　year it won't be necessary to embarrass him or her by
　　　taking a "special offering to help them on their way."
　　　Money will be there to give them an honorarium and pay
　　　their travel expenses.

B.　The Faith Promise budget should be presented to the
　　Administrative Board for its approval—assuring them that no other
　　funds of the church will be affected or used. If it does not come in,
　　it will not be spent. Once the budget has been approved it becomes
　　an official program of the church.

C.　As early as possible the Faith Promise budget should be publicized
　　to the congregation through the newsletter. This should be done at
　　least one month prior to the Missions Conference. Members should
　　be urged to pray about what God would have them do.

D.　Faith Promise Cards should be prepared. These can have the entire
　　budget printed on one side. There need not be a place for people to
　　sign. Remember, it is a covenant between them and God. He is the
　　only One who needs to know. In all my years of doing this I can
　　only remember of one year when less money came in than the
　　amount of Faith Promises that were made. The only time there is
　　ever need for the donor to sign their name is if they are wanting to
　　designate their gift.

E.　The congregation should be informed as to whether or not they will
　　be permitted to designate their gift and whether or not their desig-
　　nated gift will be prorated or will be over and above the budgeted
　　amount.

F.　The method for receiving, recording, and distributing funds should
　　be agreed upon before the Missions Conference.

IV. How to Take the Faith Promise

A.　Ideally, the Faith Promises should be taken by the pastor. He or she,
　　however, may need some coaching from the mission coordinator.
　　The missionaries should never be put in the embarrassing position
　　of appearing to be asking for money for their own support.

B. It should be done at the close of the service. (See Chapter 6, page 33, under 3.a.)
C. The Ushers should be instructed as to how to distribute and collect the Faith Promise Cards. **Advise them to be ready at the close of the service with cards in hand so as not to waste a lot of time!!!**
D. Every person in the congregation, children, youth and adults should be given a Faith Promise Card. Children are capable of making a Faith Promise. One of my grandchildren when he was a very little boy made a Faith Promise. His father reminded him that it was greater than his weekly allowance. He replied, "I know that, Dad, but didn't the preacher say we were to put down what God was telling us? Well, that is what God was telling me." He paid it! Youth have access to money either through their allowance or money they earn. They, too, should be given an opportunity to learn about God's faithfulness through Faith Promise giving. Sometimes wives want to make a Faith Promise apart from their husband or what they might do together.
E. Allow the people to have a period of prayer about their Faith Promise. While they are praying, have the organist play softly a hymn of dedication.
F. Have the ushers collect the Faith Promises, starting at the back and slowly walking toward the front picking them up as they go along. When they reach the front have a brief prayer of dedication.
G. Have someone good with figures and a calculator total them. This can be done during the singing of the closing hymn or you can have a few testimonies as to how God provided their Faith Promise this past year.
H. Announce the total. BE PREPARED TO SING THE DOXOLOGY.
I. Many churches place a large thermometer at the front of the Sanctuary with the Faith Promise goal in large letters at the top with a red ribbon which can be raised as the total is announced.

Also, sometimes a thermometer or a graph is placed on the bulletin board which show the progress that is being made in paying Faith Promises. These are the types of things that the men or youth of the church can do.

You may still have many members who do not understand the Faith Promise concept of giving. It is well, therefore, to enclose in the bulletin or even better in the church newsletter, a leaflet explaining Faith Promise giving. These can be secured from most any mission agency.

The Mission Society for United Methodists has an excellent one as does the Board of Global Ministries. One of the best we have ever seen is by Oswald Smith, entitled, "When God Taught Me To Give."

V. Sources of Faith Promise Giving

Where does the money for Faith Promise giving come from? First, let me say that I believe it is unwise to lead people to think that all they have to do is make a Faith Promise and then sit back and wait for God to provide. No! It takes a great deal of exercise of faith and much prayer. To this end I believe it is wise to place the Faith Promise Cards on the Communion Table at least once a month and urge the congregation to make them a matter of prayer. Since they have not been signed there is no fear that someone will look at them. The sources of Faith Promise funds are at least fourfold.

A. An Unexpected Source.

Very often the money will come from a totally unexpected source such as a gift, a tax refund, an unexpected increase in salary or wages. More about this later when we give examples.

B. Freed Up Money.

A second source of money for meeting our Faith Promise may be the freeing up of funds that are presently being used for something such as paying on a debt which has now been fulfilled. For example, a number of years ago we felt God was saying to us that He wanted us to commit to an additional $20 a month for the hunger of the world. We already had a sizable Faith Promise at the church and I wondered where the additional money would come from. Before the first month's payment was due I received word from the United Methodist Scholarship and Loan Fund that my daughter's obligation was paid in full. We didn't know we were that near completion for we had been paying $20 a month!

C. Money From A God Given Talent Or Skill.

Faith Promise Money may come from extra work other than our regular employment or income. One year when our daughter was a college student she had a chance to work during the Christmas holidays. The money earned enabled her to pay her Faith Promise. One lady paid her Faith Promise by baking bread, another man paid his by making and selling grandfather clocks.

D. Sacrificial Giving

Finally, meeting our Faith Promise commitment may involve an adjustment in our lifestyle. I'm not sure that we can make a Faith Promise and depend on God to provide the means to pay it while we continue to ride around in our Cadillac! A family was making a decision on the purchase of a new car. They were torn between a larger, more comfortable car (after all, they were on the road a great deal of the time!) and a smaller car with fewer frills. They finally decided to borrow the money for the bigger car, but to buy the smaller car and send the difference ($1200) to Nigeria to build housing for the students at a Pastor's Training School.

VI. Examples of Faith Promise Giving and What it has Done

A. Individuals

1. A hog farmer in northeastern Indiana made his first Faith Promise and the following year his brood sows dropped more piglets than ever before.

2. A student in Nebraska, with no visible source of income felt led of God to make a Faith Promise of $240. The next month he received a check for exactly $240.

3. An 85 year old retired school teacher who had the largest Faith Promise in her church fell out of bed and broke her hip. Upon returning from the hospital she received a check from her insurance company. She returned the check with a letter saying that the insurance company owed her nothing, that her bill had been taken care of by her hospitalization. Three times she and the insurance company exchanged checks and letters until it dawned on her, "My Faith Promise!"

4. A mission executive and former pastor and wife began their spiritual journey in Faith Promise giving in 1953 when they were chal-

lenged to make their first Faith Promise with no idea where the money would come to pay it. But God provided. With the passage of the years they watched that figure grow and grow until God challenged them to give 10% of the total Faith Promise Budget of the church they were serving at the time. Later, God challenged them to give as much for His work as they were prepared to spend for a monthly mortgage payment.

B. Churches

1. A large church in an affluent section of Western Pennsylvania was hard pressed to pay the pastor's salary and current expenses. They had not gone to conference with all apportionments paid within the memory span of any member. They were challenged to start putting missions first and began a Faith Promise program. In seven years the church was completely out of debt, their mortgage paid off, $100,000 of improvements made without borrowing a penny, a bus ministry was started, as well as hiring their own missionary to street kids, all apportionments were paid regularly, their pension indebtedness was paid in full, the pastor's salary was raised until it was the fifth highest in the conference and mission and benevolent giving multiplied ten fold!

2. A church located in a small Northwestern Pennsylvania community had planned a Missions Conference. Four months before the conference a tornado devastated the community. Of the 409 dwellings in the town 160 had been totally destroyed, 55 had major damage, another 124 suffered minor damage. Only 70 homes were left untouched. The church decided to go ahead with the Missions Conference. Their membership was 121 without a single professional person, most of the membership were blue collar workers. Their attendance was 67. They had set a goal of $5500 and the Faith Promises went to $7040 and two young persons committed themselves for full time Christian service.

3. A church in central Michigan had been a part of a two point circuit. They became a station appointment with a membership of 229 and an average attendance of 240. In their ninth Missions Conference they reached a goal of $35,000 in Faith Promise giving and 20 persons in some kind of Christian service. In the intervening years they had built a new church and parsonage, paved their parking lot and taken on a full time pastor.

4. A small church in Western Pennsylvania with a membership of 159 was the out point of a three point charge. They began a Missions Conference. Soon they became a station appointment with a full time pastor. They enlarged their church, built a parsonage, paved their parking lot and had a Faith Promise Budget of $36,000! When asked how they arrived at that figure they replied, "Simple, that is also our Current Expense Budget" They were giving dollar for dollar!

5. A small church of only 35 members in southeastern Florida was persuaded to hold an eight day Missions Conference. On the closing Sunday when the Faith Promises were taken they amounted to $10,700. And this, too, is a church with few, if any, professional or wealthy members.

"Don't Fail To Do Something Because You Can't Do Everything"

MY FAITH PROMISE
March 1998 - March 1999

Believing that the call to missions begins in the heart of God and that the supreme task of the church is to make Christ known by every means possible, I will with the help of God, give the following amount over the next 12 months. I understand that is to be in addition to the regular budget of my church.

FAITH PROMISE based on money I do not have, but for which I will trust God, giving as He gives to me, I will give: $ _____ per _____ (week, month, or year)

It may go *(please circle)* UNDESIGNATED - OR – *DESIGNATED:*
I would like to designate to the following mission projects:

1. _____   3. _____
2. _____   4. _____

Name _____   TOTAL FOR YEAR $ _____
Address_____

- Tear here & retain bottom part -
YOUR PERSONAL COPY . . .

Believing the call to missions begins in the heart of God, with the help of God, I will give the following amount over the next 12 months March 1995 - March 1996). I understand this is in addition to what I am presently giving to the regular budget of the church.
I will give: $ _____ per _____ (week, month, or year)

Designated to the following mission projects:

1. _____   3. _____
2. _____   4. _____

TOTAL FOR THE YEAR $ _____

Hyde Park United Methodist Church
500 W. Platt Street
Tampa, FL 33606

FAITH PROMISE FOR MISSIONS

This is a FAITH PROMISE*, meaning that I (we) will give the following amount in faith that God will make it possible. Since this is a covenant between myself and God, it requires no signature.

As God blesses us, I (we) will endeavor to give toward the Home and worldwide missionary program of Hyde Park United Methodist Church the following amount:

$ _____ per _____ Annual Total $ _____
This is not included in my/our normal giving to the Church Operating Budget or other commitments.

MY FAITH PROMISE FOR MISSIONS

He said to them, "Go into all the world and preach the good news to all creation. "
Mark 16:15 (NIV)

This is to remind me of my FAITH PROMISE* to my church and to God for our Home and worldwide missionary program. Since this is a FAITH PROMISE, only God and I know the amount I have faith to believe He will help me give.

$ _____ per _____ Annual Total $ _____

THIS FAITH PROMISE (Missions) pledge runs from March 1, of the current year through February 28, of the following year.

MISSIONS WORK INTERESTS

With God's help, I will make a difference in the home and worldwide missionary program by serving in the following ways:

____ Serve on a work area   ____ Participate in mission work trip
____ Host a missionary in my home   ____ Assist with Faith Promise Mission Weekend
____ Assist with food collection   ____ Pray/correspond with a missionary
____ I would like to receive a quarterly mission newsletter

Place in offering or on the altar.
Name
Address

_____
                      City   State   Zip

Chapter 12

Neighborhood Conversation Groups or "Coffees"

The neighborhood conversation group is one of the most effective means of personalizing missions. Nearly every United Methodist Church has a large group of members who will not attend a missionary service at the church. They will, however, attend an informal meeting in the home of a friend or neighbor. This is simply a case of, "if the mountain won't come to Mohammed, Mohammed will go to the mountain." We offer a few suggestions that may help to make your neighborhood conversation group more effective.

1. Set dates and times early enough to give hostesses sufficient time to invite people.
2. Choose hostesses so that the various areas of the community are represented, thus making it possible for the largest number to attend.
3. After hostesses are selected, meet with them to provide guidance as to the purpose of the meeting and the "how to" of Conversation Groups.
4. Provide hostesses with a list of church members and constituents who live in their area.
5. Remember, this is not a "ladies meeting" Make sure the men are invited also.
6. Encourage hostesses to invite neighbors who are members of other churches. This often sparks mission interest in their own church.
7. Be sure to invite neighbors and friends who may not be Christians. The Missions Conference always can be an evangelistic outreach.
8. A good time for daytime meetings to be held is 10 a.m. and 2 p.m. This gives the housewife and mother a chance to get the children off to school and get her day organized. If she chooses to come to the afternoon meeting she can be home before the children return.
9. It is well to consider having them on week nights to provide young married couples with small children a chance to attend.

10. This can be in the form of a dessert meeting starting as early as 6:30 or 7 p.m. and ending by 8 or 8:30 p.m., thus getting the children home and in bed.

11. If the Conversation Group is a dessert meeting with children invited it is well to have someone, perhaps the missionary's wife, run a separate meeting for the children in some other room such as the family room.

12. Provide baby-sitting in some room other than where the adults are meeting.

13. If the Missions Conference is to run for a week it is well to consider having your Conversation Groups meet on Monday and Tuesday evenings, thus building interest for the rest of the week.

14. Whether they are held morning, afternoon, or evening they ought not run longer than 1½ hours.

15. Be sure to start on time! Don't wait for latecomers! The missionary may have another meeting to get to. Besides, it is not fair to those who have come on time.

16. If refreshments are served (and they usually are) this should be done at the beginning. The moment someone arrives, escort them to where the food is being served. Don't wait until everyone has arrived as this can be time consuming.

17. Let people serve themselves. Avoid having the hostess bustling around looking after everyone's needs. She, too, should be a part of the group.

18. Keep food to a minimum. Remember, the object is not to eat but to fellowship with the missionary. The hostesses ought not be placed in the position of trying to out do each other.

19. It is well to consider having a Conversation Group in the home of a shut-in with someone from the church providing the food and doing the work. This does at least two things: it includes the shut-ins in the Missions Conference and it gets members of the church into the homes of shut-ins. Some shut-ins have a real prayer ministry for missions.

20. After a brief period of fellowship, introduce the missionary and give him/her about fifteen minutes to tell some-

thing about themselves and their work. Remember, very often missionaries will need guidance about how to proceed at a neighborhood Conversation Group. Don't take it for granted that they will know what to do.

21. Following the missionary's presentation open the meeting up for questions. It is a good idea for someone to be prepared with questions that should be asked.

22. If more than one missionary is present, LET JUST ONE DO THE TALKING!

23. Try to seat the missionary so that all present can see him or her.

24. Discourage the use of slides. The home does not lend itself to everyone seeing well. Also, the object of the "Coffee" is to help people become acquainted with the missionary and this is difficult in a darkened room.

25. BE SURE TO CLOSE ON TIME! Some may have to leave but are too polite to ask to be excused.

26. Close with a period of prayer. Someone who is leading the group should take the initiative to bring the meeting to a close. One of the reasons for serving the refreshments first is so the meeting can be closed with prayer. Pray for the missionary and their work, pray for the conference, pray for yourself and what your response will be to the work presented.

"The Message Takes Many Forms But It Is Always About Christ"

Chapter 13

Banners, Bulletin Boards, Displays, Flags, Maps, Posters

In this section we will be discussing the value of visuals in promoting missions. Who will create them? How, when and where to display them? What to do with them during the year?

Most anything visual is of value. For many of our members, missions is a very nebulous thing. They often have a hard time relating to missions because it all seems so far removed from them, even if it is only in the next town. This may be one reason that many people support local missions more readily than overseas missions. It is something they can see first hand. Anything that helps them more effectively relate to, and understand, the worldwide scope of missions is worthwhile.

Also, in the making of visual aids, such as banners, flags, posters, etc., is a good place to turn your people's creative ability loose! The average congregation has more skill, ingenuity and innovativeness than is ever used. The minds and imagination of the average congregation is a great untapped reservoir of inventiveness. Generally, all you have to do is tell them what you have in mind and turn them loose!

I. Banners

More and more churches are using banners as a teaching and worship tool. They also add beauty and attractiveness to the sanctuary. This is an area where folks with craft skills can make a contribution to missions that uses their ability.

Banners can be a great means of reminding people in an artistic and symbolic way of the theme of missions for that particular year. They need not be put away after the conference is over but can grace the walls of the church the entire year.

II. Bulletin Boards

Their primary function is information! Therefore, they should be placed where they can be seen by the greatest number of people. The Narthex of the church has the greatest amount of traffic on Sunday. But, the social hall or the hall leading to the church office has the most traffic during the week. Therefore, several should be placed in the church building.

Mission material placed on the bulletin board should be attractive and eye catching. When possible, information placed on the board should be large enough to be legible as someone walks by. Information should be brief and to the point. Long paragraphs usually are not read! Tidbits are better than a smorgasbord. For example, the simple statement, **Three Thousand Languages In Which There Is No Bible** is better than a paragraph of statistics.

Remember, bulletin boards are purveyors of news, not ancient history! Don't leave things on the bulletin board after they are outdated, unattractive and yellow with time. Someone on the missions committee should be in charge of the bulletin board.

III. Displays

This is an area where creativity can really go to work. What is the theme, or country of emphasis for this year? Build a display around that. Sometimes a missionary will ship you artifacts to use in a display. We had one missionary who shipped us bricks and lumber from Zaire. Even the packing crates were used to make beautiful, hardwood candle holders for the communion table of First United Methodist Church of DuBois, PA. A missionary returning home will be glad to bring home some items from the country in which he or she is serving.

If someone from the congregation is traveling overseas ask them to bring home, or ship, some things from the countries they are visiting, e.g. kimonos from Japan, a sari from India, etc.

Very often, stores will let you use mannequins or sell used ones to you cheaply. Stores are a great source of usable material. For example, a G. C. Murphy store gave us a hosiery turntable to display a huge globe that one of our men had made out of aluminum wire. The whole congregation wanted to get the world turning!

Travel agencies are a good source of colorful posters of various countries. Rummage around in attics and garages for usable items.

After the Missions Conference, don't throw anything away. Find a space in the church for storage and use it from one year to the next. It serves as a reminder to your people of what they have done in the past. But, don't keep them in storage all year. Pull them out and use them from time to time during the year.

IV. Flags

Here is an area where you might involve women of the church who feel there is nothing they can do for missions but may be excellent with needle and thread and sewing machine. Get them to make flags. I have had women make beautiful ones and it sure beats buying them.

The flags should be of countries where you are supporting missionaries, or that is a prayer focus of the church, or where there is a need for missionaries.

Missionaries can mail you a flag of the country where they are serving or bring one when they return home. This would make them of special interest.

Samples of flags can be secured from a variety of places. An embassy or consulate of a nation will often provide an authentic replica of their country's flag. Sometimes, world maps will have flags of the various countries displayed at the bottom of the map. The World Almanac is another good source for flags. Mission agencies will often have small table flags which they use for banquets.

Find a flag, or picture of a flag, small enough to place on a projector and thrown on a screen or wall and used as a pattern. A standard size for flags is 3'x5' except that a few countries have an odd shaped flag.

Flags should be displayed in the church several weeks before the conference to alert people to what is going on. They become a colorful, silent advertisement for your Missions Conference. But, flags add more than color to the sanctuary. Flags represent people, usually millions of people, many, if not most of whom, do not know the Lord.

Flags also can be a teaching tool. I often challenge young people to identify the country the flag represents and if they do I will pay the first $10 on their Faith Promise and then I add an additional dollar for every missionary they can name serving in that country. The Youth and Children do a lot better job than do the Adults.

Like the displays, flags should not be put away and forgotten until the next Missions Conference. Each month a different flag can be placed in the chancel area of the church. Information can be placed in the bulletin, giving the country they represent, the number of citizens of that country, what percentage are Christian, if any, and the names and addresses of missionaries serving in that country. People are then urged to pray for that country and the missionaries and write to the missionaries.

V. Maps

The value of maps is that they help people visualize who, what and where. Every church should have a sizable map prominently displayed in a heavily traveled area of the church. Like the bulletin board they should be conspicuous. I know of one church that has a very large map hanging on a side wall of the sanctuary. This helps remind the congregation that, "The World Is Our Parish." Political maps are best for they outline the countries in various colors.

Good sources of maps are, The United Nations, National Geographic magazine, Rand McNally stores and some Federal government offices such as the Naval Oceanographic office in Washington, D. C.

Maps are a good place to attach pictures or prayer cards and letters from your missionaries. A ribbon can be stretched from their picture to the country where they serve.

Some churches have very elaborate maps made of wood by the men of the church with a lighting system that highlights the countries of special interest to the church.

VI. Posters

What a great way to involve children. They seem to enjoy making posters. Sometimes this is turned into a contest. Children are asked to make posters depicting the theme for the conference, or their concept of missions or missionaries. What a learning experience they are for both the children and the adults. Sometimes children's insights into missions are more perceptive than adults. Posters are a good way to promote the mission theme for that year. Posters are a great way to get parents involved and out to mission meetings. They will be dragged to the church to see the poster made by their child.

Posters can line the hallways or the sanctuary walls. They, too, should not be taken down right after the conference but, perhaps, posted in the children's department of the Sunday School. They continue to be a teaching tool of the Church School. They also remind teachers that it is their job to guide and correct children in their concept and understanding of missions. Sometimes teachers need the reminder that they are training worldwide witnesses— disciples of our Lord who have also received the commission to go into all the world and preach the gospel.

Chapter 14
Music for Missions[1]

Just as music is important to any worship service, so too, it is critical to the Missions Conference or any mission emphasis service or program which the church may conduct.

I. Involve the Music Committee and Music Personnel

Be sure that the Chairperson of the Music or Worship Commission, the Organist/Pianist and Choir Director(s) are invited, yea, urged to attend any Missions Conference planning sessions. Secure their cooperation by making them feel that their contribution is important. Having them present at planning sessions avoids any misunderstandings and hard feelings.

On the other hand, while it is wrong to neglect the music, it is just as wrong to make it a major factor in the program. Music should be kept to a minimum. Save the major music program for another event in the life of the church. Remember, the purpose of the music is to prepare the people to receive the message. In fact, the music should help convey the message.

Urge the organist/pianist, song leader, choir director to make sure that all music that is used has a mission message.

II. Special Singing Groups

If there is a choral number or special solo or group number, request them to sing something that is mission oriented. Occasionally a singing group will be invited to participate in the hope of attracting a better attendance at mission meeting. This is fine except for the fact that, very often, the group providing the music will have no interest in missions and will have no mission music that they can use. Unfortunately, their presentation becomes nothing more than a performance that contributes nothing to the overall theme. It should be clearly understood that those providing music in the program will stay for the entire service, not perform and then leave.

1 See Chapter 24 "Resources for Promoting Missions in the Local Church," Music for Missions page 122.

Occasionally, choir rehearsal will conflict with a Missions Conference service. In which case, the choir should be asked to either rehearse before or after the service or postpone the rehearsal session. Ask the choir to sing on the night of their rehearsal but don't allow them to leave for rehearsal after they have sung!

III. Congregational Singing

If a song leader is used ask him or her to use only the missions numbers in the hymnal or song book. There are a number of excellent mission song books that are available for use in connection with Missions Conferences. They can be secured for a minimal price and used year after year. Also, there are some great mission words set to familiar tunes. (See Chapter 24 on Resources, page 122 Music for Missions) Take advantage of the opportunity to teach the congregation some of the good mission choruses.

IV. Piano and Organ Music

Ask the Pianist/Organist to begin playing well in advance of the start of the service. If a prelude is helpful in setting the mood for worship on Sunday morning it is helpful at the Missions Conference services. Ask that the music that is played before and after the service and during the offering (if an offering is taken) be something that strikes a familiar chord in the mind of the worshipper. A Bach chorale may be fine but, "All Hail The Power of Jesus Name," or "Jesus Shall Reign," or "Jesus Saves" is much more appropriate for a mission service.

V. Special Mission Musical Programs

It might be well to plan a major mission music program as part of the Sunday evening service, especially the first Sunday night if it is a week long conference. Occasionally one of the choirs can be persuaded to present a missions cantata. There are some excellent mission music programs for both adult and childrens choirs. (See Chapter 24 on Resources, page 124 Children and Missions)

Above all, don't let music be the tail that wags the dog. Make it contribute to, but not dominate, the missions meeting.

Chapter 15
Acquainting Children With Missions

This, apart from the chapter on prayer, is probably the most important chapter in the book. In this section we will deal with the all important business of developing a strong and interesting mission education program for children. Materials, programs and persons who conduct children's mission programs will be listed under Resources For Promoting Missions In The Local Church.

I have a friend who, when you write and invite him to a Missions Conference will inquire, "Are you going to have a program for children? If not I'm not coming."

If the harvest of recruitment is reaped in the teen years then seeds must be sown in the childhood years. It is important, therefore, that children be given an early exposure to missions.

I. How to Start

First, meet with the pastor and discuss the matter with him. Assume that he, too, is concerned about acquainting children with missions. Get his approval for a meeting with the church staff and the Sunday School teachers. Share with him programs and materials that are available.

If the church has a Director of Christian Education, plan to meet with with him or her and share with them your ideas. Ask that a meeting be set up with the children's workers and the teachers of the Children's Department of the Sunday School. Suggest that a workshop in missions for the children be conducted. Be sure that the Children's Department is represented on the Missions Committee. Work through proper channels. Don't alienate anyone. Better to consult with someone who is not involved than to miss someone who is.

II. What to Do

As we have indicated above, set up a workshop with teachers of children. Help acquaint them with programs and materials that are available.

Get the Education Committee to appoint someone as Mission Coordinator for Children. Have that person serve on the Mission Committee.

Urge that one Sunday a month be Mission Sunday. We teach the children to sing, "Jesus Loves The Little Children, All The Children Of The World." Then a Sunday a month should be devoted to helping our children know about the children of the world who don't know that Jesus loves them.

Mission Sunday can be a real educational tool by helping children better understand the customs, cultures, and religions of the world.

That Sunday can also be the day when the offering is used for some mission project which the children themselves have selected. This can also be a means of teaching about Faith Promise giving.

On that Sunday the children's department can be decorated in the motif of the country being studied. Information about location, size and needs of that country can be shared. The flag of that country should be displayed in the department. Songs that are sung should have a missionary theme. (See Chapter 24 on Resources, page 122 Music on Missions)

From time to time have the children share, in the morning worship service, what they are learning about missions. This can be combined with the Mission Moment and the Children's Sermon.

III. During Missions Conference

Certainly there should be a program for children in connection with any Missions Conference held for the general church, whether it is a one-day or week long conference.

If your Missions Conference runs during the week as from Sunday to Sunday or Wednesday to Sunday, it is possible to run a program for children after school. This, however, takes a great deal of planning and preparation. Permission has to be received from the parents for them to participate. Permission slips from the parents have to be sent to the school explaining why the children are not boarding the school bus and with whom they will be riding. Transportation has to be provided both from school to the church and from church to their home after the program is over.

There should be plenty of adult supervision. The missionary should not be responsible for maintaining discipline. Children often behave better when there is an adult present whom they know and whom they know knows their parents. There should also be someone in charge of snacks after school. Also, someone to play the piano or someone in charge of music.

Running a mission program after school requires a lot of work but it is worthwhile and can be done. The last church I served we had children in eleven different elementary schools stretched over a radius of ten miles.

Sometimes children's meetings are held in the evening and are run concurrently with the adult program. The children sometimes remain in the main assembly hall with the adults and youth for the singing and a slide or video presentation and then are dismissed for their own program in another section of the church. This, of course, requires additional ministry personnel. If you can possibly do it, it helps to engage someone who will conduct the children's mission program concurrently with your mission program. There was a time, in the recent past, when it was hard to find either material or personnel to do this but, thanks be to God that is no longer true. There is now an abundance of material being produced and many persons who specialize in children's mission programs. (See Chapter 24 on Resources for Promoting Missions in The Local Church)

If you hold evening Neighborhood Conversation Groups in connection with your Missions Conference you might consider one for young adults with children. This may be a way to get young adults out who might otherwise use the excuse that they don't want to pay a baby sitter. Advertise it as a dessert coffee. Start at 6:30 p.m. Serve dessert as soon as the first family arrives. (See Chapter 12 on Neighborhood Conversation Groups) Take the children to another area where they can be alone. Be sure the program for the adults does not run longer than the program for the children. It is very difficult for a children's worker to keep children occupied after the program is over. The entire evening program should not run beyond 8:00 p.m.

Use the children in the Missions Conference. Have them share what they have learned at some time during the conference. If your conference opens on a Sunday morning you might consider having a parade of flags with children dressed in the costume of the country whose flag they bear.

IV. Children's Mission Festival

Many churches now conduct Children's Mission Festivals separate and apart from the regular Missions Conference of the church. Usually this is at a different time of the year. It is a good way to involve young adults in the mission program of the church. There are many who would not be involved in the regular Missions Conference but they will do anything to help with the children. It is a good way to introduce missions to adults! Children's Mission Festival, like the regular Missions Conference can be of varying duration, from one day to one week. There are a number of people who specialize in conducting Children's Mission Festivals. (See Chapter 24 on Resources For Promoting Missions in The Local Church)

V. Involve and/or Acquaint the Children With the Local Mission Projects

It is not always possible for little children to be involved in or even visit some local mission projects because of the nature of the work being done. Sometimes, the persons being ministered to do not relish the idea of being stared at by little children. One has to be selective in the types of ministry to which children are exposed. At least they can become acquainted with what is going on around them.

There are, fortunately, enough mission outreach efforts of the church they can participate in. They can visit nursing homes and hospitals, or invite other children into their home. They can have a hands on experience in soup kitchens and food banks and clothing distribution. Remember the little boy in one of our major cities who gained national attention just by persuading his family to let him take blankets to the homeless in his city?

Above all, help little children to understand that they do not have to wait until they are "grown-up" to become a missionary. They can become a missionary to their schoolmates, or playmates or their own family. Sometimes I tell children if they want to see a real live missionary to look in the mirror, for anyone who loves Jesus is, or should be a missionary.

Chapter 16
Youth and the Mission Program of the Church

In this section we shall deal with involving youth in the mission program of the church through such things as the Missions Conference, Faith Promise giving, overseas visitation, and ongoing mission programs of the church.

Most missionaries receive their initial call while in their teens. Because this is true, every church should develop a strong mission program specifically aimed at the youth of the church.

Many young people receive their call to missions through contact with a visiting missionary who may have stayed in their home, or who they heard at some youth mission meeting. Another way that youth are moved to seriously consider missions as their life work is by having seen missions first hand by visiting some overseas or home mission projects as a part of a work/witness team.

They may, not feel the call of God upon heir lives for full time service, and most will not become missionaries but, by being exposed to missions in their teens, they may continue to maintain a strong interest in missions throughout their entire life. By having been touched by missions at an early age, they probably will be among the strongest supporters of missions as they assume leadership positions in the church.

I. Youth and the Missions Conference

A. Representation

Be sure to have a youth representative and a teacher or Superintendent of the Youth Department on your Missions Conference Planning Committee. Remember, the more people you can involve, the greater will be your base of support and the less indifference, hostility and opposition you will encounter.

B. Programs For Youth During The Missions Conference.

    1. The Youth Breakfast.

        Very often it is next to impossible to get youth out to evening meetings during the week what with home work, rehearsals, athletics, band, and on and on and on! Therefore, you have to

take them when you can get them. One of the times you can get
them is before school starts. It is wise, then, to plan a series of
youth breakfasts.

Often the excuse is heard that you can't get youth out that early.
Yes you can! It just takes a great deal of planning and work.
This is where your Sunday School teachers can help.
Sometimes it necessitates calling every young person in the
church. Sometimes we have called kids as early as six in the
morning, getting them out of bed and telling them that we
would be around to pick them up for youth breakfast!

a. Time Of The Breakfast. This will depend on when
    the tardy bell rings and how far the church is from the
    school. Our tardy bell rang at 8 a.m. We had young
    people in three different high schools scattered over
    the western half of the county in metropolitan
    Pittsburgh. Our breakfasts started promptly at
    7:10 a.m. and last thirty five minutes.

b. Start promptly!!! Regardless of how many kids are
    there. Have one of the young people say grace, per-
    haps one of the officers. Have the food ready to
    serve. Put the food on the table. Don't have them go
    through a cafeteria line. That takes too long. Give
    them ten minutes to eat. That is probably eight min-
    utes more than they take at home!

c. Start the program even though some of them are not
    through eating. Take a couple of minutes to line up
    transportation, making sure there are enough cars.
    Transportation is a responsibility of the
    Transportation Committee. (See Chapter 9 on
    Missions Conference Committees) This usually can
    be done by some of the older men of the church.

d. Perhaps sing a chorus, although Young People do not
    usually sing well, or enthusiastically at that hour of
    the morning. Introduce the speaker—briefly, tell the
    speaker that he or she has fifteen minutes—not six-
    teen! Promptly at 7:45 dismiss them with a brief
    prayer and load them up and send them on their way.

e. Food. Be sure to serve them a good, substantial
    breakfast. They will always eat more when they

come out to church for breakfast than they will at home. One morning at Grace Church in Oil City, PA, ninety-four young people ate over 400 pancakes. Vary the breakfast each day.

Do not charge for the breakfast. Make the cost part of your Missions Conference expense. Sometimes you can get each adult Sunday School class to take charge of one morning and they will absorb the cost of the breakfast. It is wise, however, to have one person in charge of coordinating the menu and purchasing the food.

f.　Inviting guests. Have your young people invite their friends, especially those who may not be Christians. That way, the youth breakfast becomes an evangelistic outreach. Have them invite their teachers. Even if they cannot come they will appreciate being invited and will know that something is going on.

g.　Communicate with school officials. Write a letter to the principal letting him or her know what is going on and why kids are not getting on the bus. Also, in case a carload arrives late the school officials will know why. In thirty-two years we only ever had one group late for school and that was because they got held up at a railroad crossing.

2.　Pizza Bash

If the Missions Conference is during football or basketball season it might be well to plan a pizza bash or something similar. This can be following the game. Again, they can invite their friends. Cost of the event will be absorbed by the Missions Conference budget.

This can be a time when the missionaries just sit around the table with the youth in an informal way. It can be a time when young people discover that missionaries are normal people with a sense of humor.

It should close with a challenge for missions or an invitation to accept Christ.

3.　Mission Lock-In Night.

a.　This, too, can be a Friday night affair. It may start after an evening service or after an athletic event.

This, like the Youth Breakfast, or Pizza Bash is a case of taking the young people when you can get them. Have the young people bring sleeping bags— for those who can't last the night. Have a general meeting room like a social hall but separate rooms for fellows and girls for those who want to sleep. Have plenty of sponsors or chaperones. Perhaps the night can be divided up, one group of chaperones staying part of the night and another group coming in for the last half of the night.

b.   Program. Films—on missions and, perhaps, a light comedy for entertainment. Games—the missionaries can teach them games that are played in the country in which they serve. Light conversation—the missionaries can share the humorous thing that have happened in their ministry. Challenge—around midnight, before the young people get too weary there should be a challenge for missions and to accept Christ. There should be a private place of prayer where adults can pray with young people.

c.   Food. Have plenty of snacks and soft drinks. A minimum charge can be made for soft drinks—10 cents a bottle or can just to keep the young people from overindulging or wasting. Breakfast should be served at 6 a.m., hearty and warm. Again, the expense of which should be absorbed by the Missions Conference budget. A whole different group should provide breakfast than stayed with the young people all night.

d.   No one leaves during the night unless ill. Even then, their parents should come for them or they be taken home by a sponsor. Accountability is critical!

C.   Youth And The Faith Promise.

Expect your youth to make a Faith Promise. This is one way they learn to give rather than receive. I was in a church in Delaware a number of years ago where the Youth Faith Promise came within a few hundred dollars of that of the adults— and they paid it!

They may want to select a particular project to which to designate their giving. It should be something of their own choosing, something to which they can relate.

Report the Youth Faith Promise amount in the Worship Service. Make it an important part of the service. You might have the Youth President share the platform and report.

Youth can be put in charge of an evening program. Very often they come up with innovative and creative ideas. For example at a church in Pasadena, MD they introduced all the missionaries the church was supporting—even those who were not there—by using the format of the TV program, Jeopardy. It was original, unique and humorous.

II. Work/Witness Teams and Overseas Visits

Try to involve the youth in a work team. It may be as near as one of the Conference camps or part of Habitat For Humanity project in the community. Nationally, it could be Red Bird Missions Conference in Kentucky, or Oklahoma Missions Conference, or 4-Corners Native American Ministry in New Mexico. It could be a visit to a mission project in a large metropolitan area.

Young people usually have no difficulty raising funds for this sort of thing. All they need is a little guidance and encouragement.

Encourage the sending of a young person overseas each year. This, too, can be a part of the Faith Promise Budget. (See Chapter 11 on Faith Promise Giving, page 56 Building a Faith Promise Budget)

III. Ongoing Local Involvement

Young people should be involved in some ongoing ministry in the community such as visiting shut-ins, and nursing homes, or serving in soup kitchens. Perhaps the church or community runs a coffee house or youth center in which they can become involved in an ongoing way.

IV. Year Round Emphasis

Be sure to have some kind of major mission emphasis at least once every quarter in the Sunday School and their regular youth meeting. This is one reason for having a youth representative and youth coordinator on the mission committee.

V. Helping Youth Discover God's Will

One of the ongoing questions by young people is, "How do I find God's will for my life?" or, "How do I know when it is God speaking to me?" It is well, during the course of the year to have a session or two dealing with this subject. One of the things that missionaries can talk about a Youth Breakfast or Pizza Bash, or All Night Lock In, is how they found God's will for their life.

"Any Time Is A Good Time To Do The Will Of God And Missions Is His Will."

Chapter 17

Men and the Mission Program of the Church

It is an axiom that the church's mission program is only as strong as the involvement of the men. No church will ever develop a strong missions program until the men are participating! If, for example, the membership of the church is 40% men and they are not participating or providing leadership, then it should be obvious that the church is only operating at 60% of its potential!

The question is, "How do we get the men involved?" Let's start with the Missions Conference.

I. Involving Men in Missions Conference

Be sure that the men are highly visible and utilized in the planning and program of the Missions Conference. Schedule events that are primarily, if not solely for the men.

A. Men and Missions Banquet. It is well to kick off the Missions Conference with a Men's Mission Banquet. This could be held on Saturday evening and be the starting event for the conference. Invite the strongest missionary speaker you can find to address the men. Then, hold that speaker over for your Sunday morning worship service.

It is well to sell tickets for the banquet. It is a fact that if someone purchases a ticket they are more apt to be there than if they are simply extended a general invitation. The price of the ticket need be no more than the cost of the meat. Sometimes the ladies can be persuaded to put the banquet on as part of their service to the Missions Conference. They, also, are often anxious to have the men involved. Remember, however, the purpose for selling tickets is not to make money but to assure the presence of the men at the banquet.

Make sure that every male member of the congregation is contacted and invited. If the church has a United Methodist Men's organization perhaps they will take on this task. Mine did.

B. Men's Breakfast. Another way to reach the men is through a Men's Breakfast held sometime during the conference. Very often this is on Saturday morning. Some churches do it on Sunday morning. Better to have it as early as possible so as to arouse the interest of the men in what will be happening in the church.

The breakfast can he held at a local restaurant that is frequented by the men. Better, however, to hold it at the church if possible. There the men will be surrounded by the displays and posters about the Missions Conference. You must remember that this could be the only event that they will attend and you want to get the message to them by every means possible. Perhaps the youth can be persuaded to put the breakfast on as part of their involvement in the conference.

Make sure that it's a good, substantial breakfast, not just juice and rolls and coffee. You may have some hardworking men who need a more substantial breakfast than that. You may also have some men who, for health reasons, cannot eat sweet rolls or doughnuts.

Be sure that the speaker, whether it is a banquet or breakfast, is someone who has something to say to the men. Discourage the use of slides or film at these events. Remember you are endeavoring to challenge the men as well as inform them. It is well if you can find a layman in the area who has been on a Work/ Witness Team to come and share about practical involvement in missions.

C. Displays. If possible, recruit men to help build displays and other visuals for the conference. Men are a great untapped reservoir of skills, both artistic and mechanical. Utilize what they have to offer. Sometimes they will come up with ideas that are amazing.

D. Other Ways Of Involving The Men In The Conference. Make use of the retired men of the congregation to provide such services as picking up the missionaries at the airport or hauling them to and from their other speaking engagements. Especially if it is a Round Robin Conference involving other churches. A great deal of mission cultivation can be done through these casual contacts.

Use men to transport the young people to school following the youth breakfasts, or to haul the children from school to the church for after school children's rallies and then to haul them home follow the rally.

Don't be afraid to ask the men to help prepare meals, especially ask them to be responsible for at least one of the youth breakfasts during the week. Let them put on the ladies luncheon so that the women will be free to enjoy their program without the bother of preparing and cleaning up after a luncheon.

II. Year Round Activities for the Men

Make sure that the men are involved in the year round mission program of the church. Unfortunately, many men have thought of missions only in terms of money. So much so, that they have made the two words, missions and money, almost synonymous. Help them to see that there are ways they can be involved, and things they can do that have nothing to do with money. Following are ten suggestions of things that men can do.

A. Learn the names of the missionaries, where they labor and the nature of their ministry.

B. Learn their children's names. Sometimes children are the forgotten entity of the missionary enterprise. Their happiness and adjustment on the field is vital to their parent's effectiveness. It would be great if the men would adopt a "missionary kid."

C. Do something nice for missionary children. Send them greetings on their birthday or other special occasions. Send them a subscription to a magazine such as Sports Illustrated, or Popular Mechanics, or any of the Christian Youth magazines. The women will know what magazines the girls would find interesting.

D. If they are in school in the states, invite them to spend a weekend in your home. Take them to some event in your hometown. Take them on a short vacation with you. Be a "Parent In The States" to them.

E. Help the missionary with their little problems that can be a source of minor irritation or major crisis. Help them secure parts for their car or radio or appliances. When you are 300 miles from a railroad or port and there is no local hardware store sometimes things are difficult to obtain, especially at a price they can afford.

F. Call them by phone or ham radio, or by e-mail. Phone calls overseas are easy to make and are surprisingly reasonable. Virtually every congregation has a ham radio operator. It is a great help to a missionary if they have someone who can relay messages for them.

G. Visit them when you are on vacation. Many people travel overseas these days. Be sure to secure the names and address of missionaries who serve in countries you will be visiting.

Even if you can not get to their city or station you might contact them by phone.

When you travel to Florida or California you can visit missionaries who labor in such places as Red Bird Missionary
Conference in southeast Kentucky or Four Corners Ministry
in Shiprock, New Mexico.

H. Write to them. At this point, the average man throws up his
    hands and says, "I don't even write to my kids!" You
    should! Do you have any idea what it is like to be a male
    missionary serving overseas in some out-of-the-way place
    and the only person you hear from is your Mom, or pastor,
    or missionary executive or some sweet little old lady? Men
    like to hear from men who talk their language and share
    their interests.

I. Pray For Them. If you have a Men's Prayer Group in your
    church make sure that the missionaries your church supports
    are prayed for regularly. Be sure that missionaries are includ-
    ed in your daily devotions and family prayers.

J. Talk to your children about the possibility of serving the Lord
    in some full-time capacity so that the missionary can be sure
    that if anything happens to him, his place will be filled by
    another.

III. Direct Involvement

One goal of every church should be to have its men involved in
some local mission project or ministry. Volunteer help is needed by
nearly every mission or benevolent organization. Every man should be
challenged to be directly involved in whatever is going on in their own
community or district or conference.

Further, the Faith Promise Budget should include an item to assist
persons to become part of some Work/Witness team whether overseas
or in the states. Perhaps many more people would go if they knew that
their church would assist them with the cost. To tell a young adult who
may be struggling with a mortgage and the education of their children
that he or she could go on a work crusade for $750 is not a great deal
of help. Their reply might very well be, "Yes, and I can make a mortgage payment with that amount." But, if the church will tell them that
they will invest half of the amount if they pray about God's help in providing the other half, they may give the matter serious thought.

Every church should strive to have some of its men involved every year. That way you develop a built in coterie of mission supporters and enthusiasts.

The Mission Society for United Methodists has an organization known as Christian Laymen, International which can be of help to men considering work team experiences. Also, there is, within the structure of the Mission Society an organization known as the Medical/Dental Fellowship which can be an avenue of service for those with some kind of medical experience and background. There is great need for doctors, nurses, medical technicians, veterinarians, and emergency medical experience, on Work/Witness teams.

IV. Short and Long Term Involvement

This is the age of second vocation. No longer is it necessary to spend one's life at the same job, with the same company, in the same community. Now, it is possible to have a second career. Mission agencies are looking for men and women who have reached mid-life or retirement age. And for good reasons. They probably are at the peak of performance and capability in their field or profession. They have some financial stability and security. If they have children they probably are reared and educated. If they own a home it is probably paid for. Finally, they still enjoy a measure of good health.

It is also true that mature persons adjust to cultural changes as well or better than younger people do. They have grown accustomed to change in life. They have learned to roll with the punches, to adjust to the unpredictable changes of life. Men ought to be challenged to offer themselves for short term mission work or to consider it as a second career in life.

Chapter 18

Involving Women in the Mission Program of the Local Church

Perhaps, this section is more a tribute to women than anything else.

It is said that, "Fools rush in where angels fear to tread." That is, at no time more true than when a man presumes to speak about women's involvement in missions. "Women" and "Missions" have almost been synonymous in the United Methodist Church with its United Methodist Women and predecessor organizations. But, this has its good and bad points. It is good that women have kept alive the missionary spirit and vision in many churches where there was no other missionary emphasis and activity. It is bad in that, because missions has been considered the women's sphere of activity in the church, men have tended to back off and leave the women to do it.

The total involvement of women in missions is a rather modern phenomenon. Only in the last half of the nineteenth century and all of the twentieth century has the involvement of women in missions been so extensive. Without their participation the modern missionary movement would never have been as extensive or effective as it has been. The history of Christian missions is replete with the stories of women who have been willing to go anywhere, suffer any privation and hardship, face and experience suffering, persecution and death for the sake of Christ. The eleventh chapter of Hebrews could have been written about the women missionaries of the nineteenth and twentieth centuries. No task was too menial or challenging for them to tackle for the sake of Christ. For a man to read their history is both a humbling and edifying experience. I, at least, find myself asking, "Where were the men?" "Why did the women have to do this?"

But, the question before us now is, "What is the involvement of women in the missionary outreach of the local church?" Certainly it is more than rolling bandages or making layettes for babies or baking cookies for the nursing home or preparing dinner for the Men's Mission Banquet. Not that any of these things are unimportant. Please don't stop doing them! But are there not some other things that women can be doing that would contribute greatly to broadening the church's understanding of, vision for, and commitment to missions Yes, there are! To use Elizabeth Barrett Browning's phrase in another context, "Let me count the ways."

First and foremost would be their influence on their husband and children. H. T. Maclin, former president of The Mission Society for United Methodists once told me that his grandmother prayed him into the Kingdom and on to the mission field.

Avery Manchester, once the Personnel Secretary of the Board of Global Ministries, responding to the question as to why it was so difficult to recruit missionaries in the United Methodist Church, without hesitation said, "Because missions is no longer talked about in the home or in the church." If the wife and mother of the house was talking missions certainly it would have some influence on the husband and children of the home.

The wife might encourage her husband to get more deeply involved in the mission program of the church. She might urge him or encourage him to take a mission trip, and, if possible, accompany him on such a trip. It might be that women will have to start a Mission Prayer Fellowship where missionaries only are prayed for. Here information is shared about the needs of missionaries and are prayed for. The Mission Prayer Fellowship could pray for the mission vision of the local church, the upcoming Missions Conference, the Faith Promise response of the congregation. If we believe that, "More things are wrought by prayer than this world dreams of" then the growth of the mission program of the local church could be the direct result of the Mission Prayer Fellowship.

Perhaps, one of the greatest contributions women could make to the mission program of the local church would be to occasionally say, "No" when asked to take a job around the church. To which they could add, "Find a capable man to do that!"

Women can influence the mission program of the local church by their willingness to make a Faith Promise on their own. They may have no visible means of support apart from their husband but they can trust God to provide funds out of His inexhaustible storehouse. One time my wife made her own Faith Promise and shortly thereafter she was asked to teach children suffering from cerebral palsy. God provided for her Faith Promise. Of course it goes without saying that the wife may be the one to encourage her husband to step out by faith and make a Faith Promise.

Women can also influence other women in the church. The United Methodist Women is for all the women of the church, but even so, it only exists in about half of all the United Methodist Churches and where it does it only touches an infinitesimal number of women in church. Most women, like most men, are totally untouched by the mission program of the church.

What can women do for the Missions Conference? Many of these things are so obvious that it hardly seems worth mentioning them. They can sponsor the Men's Mission Banquet. They can take charge of the Youth Breakfasts. They can help with the children's programs. I had one church where the ladies put on the mission banquet at no charge beyond the actual cost of the dinner. In one case they absorbed the entire cost of the banquet as part of their contribution to missions.

They could sponsor the weekday luncheons. A church in Greenville, PA, the ladies put on the luncheon each day of the week for the missionaries. They can sponsor a luncheon for the district preachers, their spouses and their mission chairperson. They can sponsor a luncheon for the ladies of the church and surrounding churches of the community. This can be a gala affair with things like a style show of the dress of the nations where they are supporting missionaries.

They can practice Christian hospitality by opening their home to a missionary for a meal or for housing.

Women can write letters and send birthday cards to missionaries and their children.

Women have artistic skills. They can make flags, create displays, and embellish bulletin boards.

Women, very often, are carrying the burden for volunteer work in local ministries such as soup kitchens, food pantries, clothes closets, and most local charitable organizations.

Again, to quote Hebrews, "And what more shall I say? For time would fail me to tell of..."(Hebrews 11:32) all the things in which women are, or can be, involved.

Chapter 19
Don't Forget the Shut-ins

In this section we shall be dealing with how to include your shut-ins in the mission program of the church.

Unfortunately, shut-ins are, often, one of the most neglected and overlooked groups of any church. They are remembered at Christmas and other holidays but forgotten most of the rest of the time.

Shut ins like to feel that they can still have a useful part in the life of the church. This is especially true if they were once very active members of the church.

Perhaps this period of their life can be a time of greatest usefulness. There are at least seven things a shut-in might do for the mission program of the church. Obviously, not all can do all seven but each can do something.

I. Pray

Perhaps in this way they can find their time of greatest usefulness to the Kingdom. They have the time to pray, and, very often, are experienced in prayer. Ask them to pray about the missionary program of the church, to pray for the Missions Conference, to pray that God will raise up harvesters to take their place in the harvest field of the Lord.

I once had a missionary friend who had served many years under the Board of Global Ministries in Mozambique. Her name was Victoria Lang. She was confined to her room in a United Methodist nursing home. She was blind, but she had a large album with pictures of missionaries for whom she prayed regularly. She once told me that she prayed for me everyday— that is both humbling and heartening!

Share with them the needs of missionaries so that they can pray intelligently. Ask them to pray for the youth of the church that they will find God's will for their lives. Give them the names of specific missionaries for whom to pray. Be sure they receive the missionary's prayer letters.

II. Write

Many shut-ins send cards to family and friends. It is their way of staying in touch. Suggest to them that they include the missionaries and their children on the list of those with whom they correspond. They can be come a kind of second grandparent, sending birthday greetings and cards on special days.

III. Host

They can host a neighborhood conversation group or prayer group. (See Chapter 12 pertaining to Neighborhood Conversation Groups.)

IV. Use the Phone

We always had our shut-ins call the entire membership, inviting them to attend the Missions Conference or any other special meeting that were being held in the church. Assign them a couple pages of the membership list and let them do the calling at their leisure or when they felt up to it. It is a way to help them keep in contact with the membership of the church. It also helps the membership to realize that they have not been to see a shut-in in a long time. Besides, it is awfully hard to say no to a shut-in!

V. Use Their Skill, Talent or Abilities

Many shut-ins, have skills or talents that they can use for the work of the Lord. They may be able to sew, or make posters or bake cookies for the fellowship hour following the meetings. Sometimes they are just waiting to be asked to do something and feel left out when they are not asked.

VI. Committee Members

They can serve on a committee even if they never attend the meetings. Consult them for their advice, draw on their wisdom. Maybe they can write up the minutes of the meetings. Make them feel they are a part of what is going on at the church.

VII. They Can Give

The shut-ins should be given an opportunity to make a Faith Promise. After all, God is able to channel funds through a shut-in as well as an active member of the church. Many shut-ins have access to funds they are not presently using. They, too, may have their alabaster jar of precious perfume which when broken and poured over the Body of Christ can send its fragrance all over the world. Don't underestimate the ability of your shut-ins to give.

Finally, many missionaries are willing to accompany the pastor to call on the shut-ins. They are willing to show their slides or video of their work. This is truly a labor of love but be sure to ask the missionary if he or she is willing to do it.

Chapter 20

A Year Round Mission Program for the Ideal Church

This section will deal with ways of keeping missions before your people all year long and not just during the annual Missions Conference.

If we believe that worldwide witness is **the** business of the church then it ought not to be limited to a brief period in the life of the church but should be a year long emphasis. It is not the special concern of a small committee or a group of spiritually elite but is, or should be, the concern of the entire church. How to attain the goal of total involvement of the total membership requires careful, continuous planning and promotion and a great deal of prayer.

First, as Andrew Murray points out in his excellent book, **Key to the Missionary Problem**, the pastor is the key to the mission effectiveness of the church. He must firmly believe that missions is the business of the church and let his people know that. He must ardently and enthusiastically work at it. Generally, the vision of the congregation is no higher than the vision of the pastor. They are going where he is going.

I. Morning Worship

A year round mission emphasis should start where everything starts—with worship. At least one Sunday a quarter the worship service should be on a mission theme. There is enough Biblical material so their should be no shortage of subject matter.

The music; prelude, congregational singing, choral anthems or solos, offertory and Postlude should all be on missions. There are plenty of mission hymns in the average hymnal that it should not be necessary to repeat all year long.

The pastor's message should be on missions. The liturgical calendar and the lectionary provide ample opportunity for preaching on mission themes. What better opportunities for mission preaching than Advent, Christmas, Lent, Holy Week, Easter, and Pentecost!

At least once a month there should be a Mission Moment in the worship service. This is an excellent way to give the congregation an update on missions, share something from a missionary prayer letter, or remind them of upcoming mission programs. It also helps to remind the congregation, without even mentioning it, to pray about their Faith Promise. We always placed the Faith Promise cards on the Communion Table once a month and urged the congregation to pray about them. This was easy to do since we never asked our people to sign them.

The flag of the country where one of the missionaries is serving and that the church supports, should be placed in the chancel area each month. Some information about the country, its needs, and the name and address of the missionary, or missionaries serving there should be placed in the bulletin and the congregation urged to pray for and write that missionary.

II. Sunday Evening Service

If the church has a regular Sunday evening service it is an excellent time to celebrate missions. It can be an informal, informational, inspirational time devoted to praise for what God is doing in the world. It is a great time to learn new mission songs and choruses.

It can also be a time when local mission ministries are presented to the church. We need not wait until annual Missions Conference to promote local mission agencies. Since they are local they can be invited most any time to share about their ministry. This can be done at minimal cost since little travel is involved.

Sunday evening is also a good time for the showing of mission films or videos that the missionary may have sent.

III. Prayer Meeting and/or Bible Study

If the church has a Bible study is good to devote one quarter a year to studying the Biblical basis for missions. Missions really is the message of the Bible from Genesis to Revelation. The Bible is the record of God seeking His errant children. It is an inexhaustible source of teaching material on missions. Perhaps an interesting study would be Missions In The Psalms.

If the church has a midweek prayer service at least once a month the prayer time can, specifically and pointedly, be for missions and missionaries. It is also a good time to pray for the local church's vision and burden for the world. It is a great time to pray for God to raise up harvesters from the congregation.

IV. Sunday School

There was a time when the fourth Sunday of the month was mission Sunday. Unfortunately about all that was ever done was designate that Sunday's offering for missions. That certainly was better than nothing but little was done on that Sunday to promote missions in the Sunday School. The Sunday School is an excellent avenue for promoting missions especially in the children and youth departments. Regretfully, in the average United Methodist Church the adult department has shrunk to the point where there are relatively few adult members of the church who attend Sunday School. But, for those who do, advantage should be taken of the opportunity to promote missions.

Since Sunday School is about Bible study it provides an excellent opportunity for helping persons of all ages understand the Biblical mandate. It is in the Bible that we find Purpose, Motivation, Principles, Methods and Techniques for missions. Therefore, the Bible is our best and primary source of mission inspiration and guidance.

Fortunately, there is now an abundance of mission material for children. At one time, in the recent past, that was not true but now there is. (See Chapter 24 on Resources For Promoting Missions in the Local Church, page 124 Children's Material & Workers)

Each Sunday School class should adopt a missionary or mission project for special emphasis by that Class. On Mission Sunday information can be shared, cards signed by the class and time spent in prayer for the missionary.

V. Fellowship Dinners

There is no reason why the International Dinner should be limited to the Missions Conference. Why not a dinner from time to time which highlights the country where one of your missionaries is serving. Write and ask them for recipes of food typical of that country. Decorate the Social Hall in the theme of the country. Hang the flag of the country. If there was a display of that country in your Missions Conference, get it out and use it. Play music typical of the country. Play a taped message from the missionary. Let him be the speaker by cassette tape or video. Perhaps have a phone hookup with the missionary that evening.

VI. Coordinate the Mission Program of the Entire Church

One of the reasons for having a broad spectrum of the church represented on your Missions Task Force is so that the entire mission program of the church will all be going the same direction. Try to get the women's organization of the church, by whatever name it goes under, to be a part of what the entire church is doing. It is not wise to have various groups in the church doing their own thing. It actually weakens the effectiveness of the church's mission program.

VII. Books on Missions for the Church Library

The average church library is woefully lacking in books on missions. Unfortunately that is also generally true of the average Christian bookstore.

From time to time highlight a good book on missions. If someone offers to place a book in the library in memory of a relative or friend ask if it could be a recent book on missions. Vary the books. From time to time let it be a history of Christian missions, or biography of a missionary, or trends in missions, modern mission problems and "How To" books on mission promotion. (Under Chapter 24, Resources For Promoting Missions, we will share information about sources of good books on missions.)

VIII. The Church Newsletter

The church newsletter is an excellent way to assure that missions will have a year round emphasis in the church. It is a good place to share excerpts of missionary letters. From time to time give the congregation an update on their Faith Promise giving and what it is accomplishing. This is also a good place to give statistics and updated information on world missions. While people do not long remember statistics at least they make a impression on them. For example, this is the place to tell them such things as the fact that 95% of all Christian dollars are spent on 5% of the worlds population. Ask for a missions corner in the newsletter.

IX. Exploding Myths About Missions

This is an ongoing task in the church. The average American Christian entertains some humorous, pathetic and tragic myths about missions. Very often their understanding of missions is right out of the nineteenth century.

Even the word missionary has a strange connotation in the minds of many. When the word, "missionary" is mentioned they will conjure up in their mind a man with a pith helmet plodding through the jungle with a stream of natives following behind, carrying his gear.

Or they may think of a spinster who missed God's best for her life—married with children and a successful career—seated by a camp fire with a group of half clad native children gathered around her listening to a Bible story or learning to sing a hymn from another culture.

In today's world, nothing could be further from the truth. Jungles are disappearing at an alarmingly rapid pace. People live in megacities. Sometimes their culture and education are superior to ours. Sometimes their economic status is equal to or higher than ours. We do not go to them because they are "poor, unfortunate, uneducated savages." We go because they need to hear of the love of God whatever their cultural, educational or economic status may be. We go because He wants us to go!

Promoting mission throughout the year helps dispel some of these myths by using a variety of teaching tools.

X. Broadening Their Comprehension

It might be well for a church to enhance the congregation's mission IQ by publishing an abridged mission vocabulary so than when a missionary comes to the church they will better understand some of the things he or she is saying. It will also help them in any mission reading they may do. It is most unfortunate when, even in the most mission minded church a member could respond to the question, "What is the Great Commission?" by replying, "It is the salary we pay missionaries!"

Some examples of vocabulary that would help our congregation's comprehension:

1. **A Call** - Discovering God's will for our life.
2. **A Candidate** - One who has been accepted by a mission agency.
3. **Contextualization** - (A fifty cent word!) Explaining the gospel in terms the local culture can understand.
4. **Cross Cultural Evangelism** - Going from one culture to another where there is not now an established church.
5. **Culture Shock** - What a missionary experiences when he goes to a culture different from his own. Or, when he returns home!
6. **Deputation** - Developing prayer support, raising funds, answering innumerable questions.

7. **Hidden People or Unreached People** - People who have not yet had the privilege of hearing the Good News.
8. **Indigenous** - A church whose leaders and members are nationals of the country where the church exists. It means the church has been planted.
9. **Missionary** - A bearer of Good News. Strange that this should need to be explained to people.
10. **Paternalism** - Thinking that our culture is superior. That our way of doing something is better than those to whom we go.
11. **Syncretism** - The blending of paganism and Christianity i.e. Christianity mixed with voodoo.
12. **Tentmakers** - Those who have a secular or governmental job but while they are in another country they really know they are representatives of Jesus Christ.

This is but a sampling of words common in mission parlance today. They reveal the necessity of mission education and promotion as a year round task of the church.

Chapter 21

The Care and Feeding of Missionaries

Your missionary wants to be as effective as possible. You can help him or her by considering the following.

REMEMBER: Missionaries are the Lord's servants sharing with you what Christ is doing in the area where they serve. They can do this best when they are at their best! They want to be used of God to inform, inspire and challenge. Remember, they may be lonely and weary; away from home and on the road for long periods of time; trying to maintain a high level of enthusiasm and spiritual vitality as they move from church to church. You can help them by giving them some things that money can't buy.

WRITE: Communicate with the missionary, asking about the following things. Allow plenty of time for a reply. Remember they may be on the road and it may take a while for correspondence to catch up with them.

PROGRAM: Let them know the nature of your program and what you hope for from them. This will give them plenty of time to prepare. If you expect them to show slides or a video, tell them exactly how much time they will have and let them know they will be expected to keep within the time limit. Be sure to ask about equipment needs.

Remember, also that most missionaries, like most pastors, are one or two talented people. Not all do all things well. Ask them what they do best, or what they are most comfortable doing. Many are not strong pulpiteers. Some are frightened of children. Some are effective with youth. Some are at their best with small conversation groups. **Always remember that their ability as a mission interpreter may be no indication of their effectiveness as a missionary!**

FOOD: For the missionary food is an occupational hazard. It is one of their biggest problems when doing deputation work. Do not expect them to eat like a horse and preach like St. Paul. Even St. Paul could not do that! Ask about any health or diet problems. Be sure to inform their hostess so that no one will be embarrassed.

If missionaries are to be entertained in homes, have the hostesses coordinate their meals. Don't give them ham every day for a week. If they are to eat noon and evening meals in different homes, make sure that one of the meals is light. Let them know, as graciously as possible, that no one will be offended if they do not take second helpings. If you ask what they would like for breakfast and they tell you one slice of toast and a half cup of coffee, then that is what to give them. Try to honor their wishes. Do not serve them anything without asking. Most missionaries have eaten scads of food they didn't like just to avoid offending. It is bad enough to have to do that on the field, but not on furlough! If a service is to follow a meal, allow plenty of time in between.

Don't overdo! Most missionaries would prefer to eat whatever you would ordinarily serve your own family. You may not kill them with kindness but you may make them feel mighty uncomfortable.

HOUSING: Ask what they prefer for housing. Most missionaries are glad to be housed in a private home Others, because of health problems, might find that embarrassing and would prefer a motel, even if they have to pay for it themselves.

Try to provide for privacy. People who are in public much of their life welcome moments of private relaxation. Give them a place where they can work and relax. They may have much writing or studying to do. Ask about needs such as typewriter or work table. Sometimes a room at the church can be used for work and study.

If they are to itinerate in an area, as in a Round Robin Missions Conference, try to keep them in the same house. Don't ask them to move from home to home. Ask the church in which they are to speak to arrange for their transportation to and from. Missionaries doing deputation work get awfully tired of packing and unpacking their suitcase!

Preachers usually enjoy the fellowship of the missionary, but sometimes it is better to house them with a parishioner for the sake of the contacts they may make. Besides, the parsonage hostess may need a rest. Don't feel you must be entertaining the missionary. Don't expect to be entertained by them!

TRANSPORTATION: Inquire as to how they will be traveling. If they are flying, arrange for someone to meet their flight. It is an awful feeling to step off a plane and find no one to meet you. Invariably you ask yourself, "Now what do I do?" If they are driving, give them **explicit directions** as to how to find the church. In describing how to find the church, remember, everything is familiar to you — nothing is to them. If possible, draw a map of the area in which the church is located.

Be sure to ask what their travel expenses are. Remember that expenses are more than just mileage or airline tickets. There are restaurants and motels enroute. Try to have a check ready for them before they leave. Some missionaries operate on a very close budget.

Don't embarrass them by asking about an honorarium. If you can give one, do it. Always err in the direction of generosity. Sometimes this is a way that missionaries do their Faith Promise giving.

MEAL AND SPEAKING SCHEDULES: Have ready to give to cach missionary upon arrival a schedule of their speaking assignments and the where and with whom they are to take their meals. On the speaking schedule indicate the type, time and place of the meeting. If it is to be a Neighborhood Conversation Group, give the name, address, and phone number of the hostess. It is well if the host and hostess can arrange to have someone pick the missionary up at the church or the home where they are staying.

AFTER THEY LEAVE: Bc surc to write them a letter of thanks, regardless of what kind of job they did, whether good or bad, at least they gave their time. The missionary likes to know that his or her efforts have been appreciated.

PRAYER: I've saved the most important until last! Missionaries both need and depend on your prayers. Let them know you are praying for them—before they come, while they are with you and after they leave. Remember, missionaries are very human, having the same needs and problems as you. <u>PRAY FOR THEM</u>!

**"Crossing The Sea Does Not Make You A Missionary,
But Seeing The Cross Does."**

Chapter 22

How to Write a Letter to a Missionary

"As cold water to a thirsty soul,
so is good news from a far country." Proverbs 25:25
(Especially if that "far country" is home!)

This section will deal with what seems to be one of the most difficult things that most people do, especially men, and that is write a letter to a missionary. It will also deal with little ministries to missionary children.

One of the things we usually ask people to commit to is to **write at least one letter a year to a missionary**. When this suggestion is made the usual response is, "But, I don't know what to say." What would you say if you were writing to a friend? Say some of the same things. It need not be long and formal. Give them good news. If the church has just completed a successful Missions Conference share that. If the missionary is included in your Faith Promise budget, tell them that.

If this is a first ever letter, let them know a little about yourself. Tell them what you do for a living, what your church involvement may be. You don't need to tell them your age but you can give them some idea by telling them such things as how many grandchildren you have. (Don't brag on your children or grandchildren!) Perhaps; you can send them a picture. If you are writing for a Sunday School class or group in the church, send a picture of the group. Try to include a little humor. Share a recent joke you heard. Don't make it gloomy! Don't make it an eleven o'clock news report with all the murder, rape and child abuse in your community.

Be sure to ask to be put on their mailing list to receive their prayer letters. If you have read one of their prayer letters, mention something they may have said. I once wrote a missionary in Kenya, Africa and mentioned something he had said in his last letter. He responded **immediately** saying, "Praise the Lord! Someone read my prayer letter!" If you have a prayer need share that with the missionary. They, too, want to pray for their supporters.

Don't be alarmed or upset if you don't get a personal letter back from the missionary immediately. Remember he has many demanding duties on the field and many with whom to correspond. Don't feel hurt if you get a printed or photocopied letter from the missionary. It is their way of staying in touch. My wife used to say that she looked upon the missionary's prayer letter as their personal letter to her which they were sharing with a lot of other people.

Be careful what you put in a letter. Never, NEVER, **NEVER** put cash in a letter going overseas. It is not even wise to put checks in a letter. Ask if the missionary has bank account here in the States in which gifts of money can be deposited. Or, ask the mission agency to get it to them. Most mission agencies allow their missionaries to accept monetary gifts on birthdays, anniversaries or Christmas. All other money usually must be reported to the agency and credited to their account.

Small things sometimes can be put in an envelope. I have a friend who, if blessed by a daily devotional, tears the page out and sends it to a missionary friend. One missionary shared how blessed she was when someone, in the Fall, send her three maple leaves in a letter— a poignant touch of home!

Don't forget that missionaries have children. When writing, inquire about them. If they are in school away from home, whether in the States or some overseas missionary school, ask if there is anything they need or that you can send them.

Get the names, ages and birthdays of the children. Send them a card on their birthday. If possible, subscribe to a magazine for them. Inquire about their favorite sports team and send them clippings of their activities and accomplishments. This is a good activity for a men's group. Send them little things. I remember one time when a member of my church was shipping a diesel part to Zaire and around it he packed, instead of paper or plastic he filled the carton with strips of suckers. The missionary wrote back saying that while they were glad to get the diesel part, they were thrilled to get the suckers!

Be careful about sending packages. Before you do, check with the missionary or mission agency. Sometimes the duty is more than the item is worth. The missionary can get things where he or she is stationed and don't have to pay duty on them.

Don't forget the telephone! Many missionaries have a phone, especially in some of the more advanced countries like Japan. It is surprising how inexpensive an overseas phone call can be.

If you are traveling in a country, check before you leave and see who the missionaries are serving; in that country. If possible call on them or at least call them by phone and let them know of your presence in their country. It is always good to be remembered.

Chapter 23

Missions Coordinator and/or Missions Work Area Chairperson Duties/Responsibilities

Believing as we do that the business of the Church is worldwide witness, the task of the Missions Coordinator is one of the, if not the most important lay task of the church. It must be undertaken, therefore, by someone who truly believes that this is, not just one of many tasks in the church, but, the main business of the church.

It shall be the responsibility of the Missions Coordinator to devise and develop every possible means of promoting interest in, and support for, the mission program of the local church. The Missions Coordinator, therefore, shall act as liaison between the missionaries and the local congregation; informing, inspiring and challenging.

PRAYER

The most important task of the Coordinator is to develop a prayer ministry for missionaries, mission projects, and the Unreached Peoples of the world. This might be done by:

1. Organizing Missionary Prayer Groups which meet regularly to pray specifically for missionaries and their needs.
2. Publishing in the Bulletin each Sunday a missionary for whom the Church will be praying that week.
3. Share with the entire church the prayer needs of the missionaries. This might be done through the church newsletter.
4. Flash the picture of the missionary on the wall, much as we do for choruses, and take a moment to pray for them.
5. Work toward having every member committed to praying regularly for a particular missionary or mission project.
6. Share Biblical passages about praying for missionaries.

INFORMATION

Keep the congregation informed as to what God is doing in the world through those who represent us in fulfilling the Great Commission. This could be done by:

1. Sharing bits from the missionary newsletters the church receives.
2. Have a mission minute in the morning worship service at least once a month.
3. Once a month, in the church newsletter, share information about one of the countries where your missionaries are laboring.
4. Place a mission bulletin board and/or a map of the world in the Narthex of the church.
5. Include a brief biographical sketch of a missionary family in the bulletin or church newsletter each month.

COMMUNICATION

1. Write, WRITE, **WRITE** to the missionaries.
2. Urge every member, **especially the men**, to write at least one letter a year to a missionary.
3. Get the children to write letters or send picture or tapes with greetings to missionary children, especially on their birthdays or special days.
4. Share these special times with the congregation.
5. Remember the missionaries, **and their children**, on special days such as Christmas, Easter, Birthdays, etc. Surprise them with a special gift from time to time.

PROMOTE

1. Take advantage of every opportunity to promote missions in every Sunday School class and at every church function whether it be social or spiritual.
2. Develop some means of visually reminding the congregation that missions is the most important business of the church.
3. Make greater use of flags of countries where you have missionaries laboring as a means of education and information.
4. Adopt an annual theme for missions for the local church.
5. Make missions an important part of Vacation Bible School and Sunday School.
6. Encourage the children in Sunday School to have their own mission project.

7. Have the children visit some local mission project.
8. Involve the children in ministry in nursing homes or Toys For Tots.
9. Encourage the children and youth to make a Faith Promise and do some sacrificial giving. (**Of course the adults will have to set the example of sacrificial giving.**)

REPORT

1. Give the congregation a monthly report of their Faith Promise Giving.
2. Report what is being accomplished through their giving.
3. Report of the accomplishments of the missionary or problems they face.
4. Report on what is happening in and through the Church worldwide.

RECRUIT

1. Promote missions as a career possibility for Children, youth and adults. Let children know that it is not too early to begin to think about missions. Let adults know that there are "second career" possibilities.
2. Inform the congregation of the missionary personnel needs of organizations which the church supports through its Faith Promise Giving.
4. Send some young person to visit an overseas mission project every year. This could be a part of the Faith Promise Budget or a youth project.
5. Organize a work/witness team every year to go somewhere in the world.

GOAL SETTING

Set some mission goals for the church other than financial. However, be sure to set a financial goal. **Remember, the best way to hit nothing is to aim at nothing!** Such goals might include:
1. Every member involved in writing a letter to a missionary
2. Every member praying regularly for a missionary.
3. Every member involved in some local mission project.
4. Every member reading at least one book a year on missions.

5. Call a missionary on the phone each month—it is easier than you think.

6. Have some sort of major mission emphasis in the church at least once every quarter. Don't make the annual Missions Conference the only major mission emphasis.

All of the above is more than one person can do. There should be a strong, working committee but someone should be in charge to see that it gets done. It should also be recognized that nothing is done without consultation with the pastor and the approval of the administrative board.

You will note that we have said nothing about the annual Missions Conference. This is a whole other area of responsibility that requires more space and consideration than these two pages.

Chapter 24

Resources for Promoting Missions in the Local Church

This list of suggested resources is in no way intended to be an exhaustive reference library of books, periodicals and organizations that might be helpful to the average pastor or layperson. It is, rather, a short list of things that they may find helpful.

Nor have I attempted to give a list of books on various mission subjects. They are apt to be outdated before this goes to press. I am, however, suggesting some types of books that would be helpful and ought to be in every church library. I have also listed the sources of such books. Unfortunately, the average Christian bookstore carries few to none of the current books on missions. They can order them for you if you give them author, title and publisher.

For the person really interested in missions they ought to have a good book on the Biblical theology of missions, a history of Christian missions, something on modern mission problems and, perhaps, a good book on comparative religions. It would be helpful to have something on culture and the problems a missionary faces in interpreting the gospel in a culture other than his own...Be sure to have some good books on mission motivation.

There are several books that are almost a must. I list three of them here:

Books

Mission Handbook
Edited by John A. Siewert and John A. Kenyon
Published by MARC
(The primary purpose of this book is to provide the reader with ready access to vital and current information on Christian mission agencies based in North America and engaged in overseas ministries.)

Concise Dictionary Of The Christian World Mission
Edited by Stephen Neill, Gerald H. Anderson, and John Goodwin
Published by Abingdon Press
(This is an attempt to provide in dictionary form comprehensive information to the process through which Christianity has grown from a western to a universal religion.)

Operation World
Author: Patrick Johnstone
Published by Zondervan
(This book is a day-by-day guide to praying for the whole world.)

Periodicals

In addition to a few basic books, every pastor and local church mission leader should be receiving some periodicals which will keep them abreast of what God is doing in His world today. Several such are listed below.

Evangelical Missions Quarterly
Published by Evangelical Missions Information Service, Inc.
P. O. Box 794
Wheaton, Illinois 60189
708-653-2158

International Bulletin Of Missionary Research
Published by Overseas Ministries Study Center
4490 Prospect Street
New Haven, Connecticut 06511-2196

Mission Frontiers
Published by the U.S. Center for World Missions
1605 Elizabeth Street
Pasadena, California 91104
818-398-2236

Mission Today: An Annual Overview Of World Missions
Published by Berry Publishing Services, Inc.
701 Main Street
Evanston, Illinois 60202
708-869-1573

World Pulse
Published by Evangelical Missions Information Service, Inc.
P. O. Box 794
Wheaton, Illinois 60189
708-653-2158

Organizations

Below are listed a number of organizations that are a good source
of books and materials.

Advancing Churches In Missions Commitment (ACMC)
P. O. Box ACMC
Wheaton, Illinois 60189
708-260-1660

Evangelical Fellowship Of Mission Agencies (EFMA)
1023 15th Street NW Suite 500
Washington, D. C. 20005
202-789-1011

Church Growth Book Club
533 Hermosa Street
South Pasadena, California 91030
818-305-1280

Missions Advanced Research And
Communication Center (MARC)
121 East Huntington Drive
Monrovia, California 91016-3400
818-303-8811

Service Center, General Board Of Global Ministries
7820 Reading Road - Caller No. 1800
Cincinnati, Ohio 45222-1800

United Nations Publications
Room DC2-0853
New York, New York 10017
(A good source of flag kits and information
about the nations of the world.)

U. S. Center For World Missions
1605 East Elizabeth Street
Pasadena, California 91104
818-398-2236

William Carey Library
P. O. Box 40129
Pasadena, California 91114
800-777-6371

Music for Missions

Missionary Message In Song by Eugene L. Clark
Published by Back To The Bible Broadcast
P. O. Box 82808
Lincoln, Nebraska 68501
402-474-4567

Also, Eugene Clark has produced some excellent Cantatas for
Mission written and produced for the average volunteer choir:
> *The Greatest Story Yet Untold*
> *Let The Earth Hear His Voice*
> *The Last Commandment*
These also are available from Back To The Bible Broadcast

Missionary Words And Tunes
Compiled by Evelyn McIntosh
China Outreach Ministries
P. O. Box 2737
Boca Raton, Florida 33432
561-852-8759
(This is a collection of mission songs and choruses,
many of them set to familiar tunes.)

Many of the mission agencies have leaflets of mission songs and they can be had simply by writing to the mission agency.

Audio Visual Materials

All of the mission agencies have materials available that can be obtained simply by writing them. Many are free but some have a rental fee. Several excellent sources of films and cassettes are:

Moody Institute Of Science
820 North LaSalle Boulevard
Chicago, Illinois 60610-3284
312-329-2190

World Vision International
121 East Huntington Drive
Monrovia, California 91016-3400
818-303-8811

Wycliffe Bible Translators, Inc.
P. O. Box 2727
Huntington Beach, California 92647
714-969-4600

Children's Material and Workers

Until relatively recently there were few persons who worked with children in missions and next to no material. Today, thank God, there is a plethora of both. We list some of both below.

Child Evangelism Fellowship
2300 East Highway M.
Warrenton, Missouri 63383
314-456-4321

Children's Mission Resource Center
U. S. Center For World Mission
1605 Elizabeth Street
Pasadena, California 91104
818-398-2233

Catalogues and Worldview Packett
Kids Can
4445 Webster Drive
York, Pennsylvania 17042
800-KIDS-554

Children And Youth Packet
Mission Education ACMC
P. O. Box ACMC
Wheaton, Illinois 60189-8000
312-260-1660

Kids For The World
Gerry Dueck
William Carey Library
P.O. Box 40129
Pasadena, California 91119

Missions Curricula For Children Grades 1-6
Crossroads Communications
P. O. Box 111475
Campbell, California 95011
408-378-6658

Missions Made Fun For Kids
Elizabeth Whitney Crisci
Accent Publications
P.O. Box 33640
Colorado Springs, Colorado 80936

The Mission Society For United Methodists
6234 Crooked Creek Road
Norcross, Georgia 30092
800-478-8963

World Focus Series and World Children's Calendar
Monarch Publishing Company
245 2nd Avenue NE
Milaca, Minnesota 56353

Below are listed some excellent children's workers who are available for your Missions Conference or to put on a Children's Mission Festival.

Mrs. Pamela Downs
Mission Society For United Methodists & Renew
4055 Ebenezer Road
Marietta, Georgia 30066
404-591-7310

Luella Krieger
114 East Main Street
Sykesville, Pennsylvania 15865

Rev. and Mrs. Charles Shearer
China Outreach Ministries
2005 Market Street Extension
Middletown, Pennsylvania 17057
717-939-4738

Mr. and Mrs. William Taylor
1009 Plato Avenue
Orlando, Florida 32809
407-851-6470

Mrs. Robert Walz
China Outreach Ministries
P. O. Box 370
Fairfax, Virginia 22030
703-273-3500

Mrs. Nancy Mabrey
Gospel Illusion and Chalk Message
Wesley Memorial United Methodist Church
P.O. Box 2558
Lake City, Florida 32056-2558
904-752-3513

Youth

Below are listed several organizations which can be useful to you in helping young people find God's perfect will for their life. Most of the mission agencies have youth mission ministries and overseas work/witness teams. Many of the mission agencies have short term mission opportunities for youth. Information can be secured simply by writing to the mission agency.

Campus Crusade For Christ, International
100 Sunport Lane
Orlando, Florida 32809
407-826-2000

Intercristo
19303 Fremont Avenue, North
Seattle, Washington 98133
800-251-7740

InterVarsity Missions
P. O. Box 7895
Madison, Wisconsin 53707-7895
608-274-9001

Youth For Christ USA/World Outreach Division
P. O. Box 228822
Denver, Colorado 80222-8822
303-843-9000

Youth With A Mission (YWAM)
P. O. Box 55309
Seattle, Washington 98155
206-363-9844

Some Do's and Don'ts

1. Do pray about everything.
    Don't neglect prayer.

2. Do Trust God to do what seems humanly impossible.
    Don't doubt.

3. Do plan early and well.
    Don't overlook anything.

4. Do have a good, well rounded committee.
    Don't overlook any group in the church.

5. Do plan your program to reach every age group.
    Don't leave anyone out.

6. Do check your committee's progress.
    Don't procrastinate.

7. Do set some goals.
    Don't be alarmed if you don't reach your goals.

8. Do emphasize people more than money.
    Don't be afraid to mention money—Jesus did.

9. Do have high expectations for your people.
    Don't let pessimism frighten you.

10. Do be willing to be innovative.
    Don't be afraid of failure.

11. Do have continuity.
    Don't feel you must do something a certain way.

12. Do let your program grow.
    Don't try to do everything the first year, or second year,
    or third year.

13. Do emphasis mission throughout the year.
    Don't limit missions to one day or one week, or
    one month.

14. Do be confident, remember, it is His work.
    DON'T GET DISCOURAGED!

Chapter 25

The Local Church: The Ultimate Mission Sending Agency

I include this address, given at the Good News Convocation in Abilene, Texas on June 29, 1982, simply to help the local church recover and appreciate the importance of its roll in the glorious task of making Christ known to His world.

The local church. One of the most maligned, criticized, ignored and ridiculed institutions in all the world. Jokes about the local church are legion. Probably no where else are the foibles and frailties of mankind more evident than in the local church. Perhaps this is because it is the only place where all our actions are viewed against the backdrop of the Word of God and measured by the perfection of Jesus.

God, however, has paid the local church the highest of compliments by assigning to it the greatest of tasks, that of making known to the world the unsearchable riches of His grace as revealed in Jesus Christ.

Unfortunately, the local church has had a very narrow view of its task and purpose in the world. It has often been criticized for being self-centered and parochial, with little understanding of the nature and magnitude of the job it faces. It sees itself as a worshipping community rather than a witnessing fellowship. I would remind you the Order Of Service for the Reception of Members opens with the words, "the Church is of God and will endure until the end of time for the conduct of worship" and ends with the words, "and the conversion of the world."

Eric Alexander, the Scottish Presbyterian preacher, has pointed out that, "Worship and missions are so bound together in the economy of God that you really can't have one without the other." In fact, he puts it even stronger and says, "Worship without a mission burden is humbug." Yet it is a rare church that has budgeted as much to make Christ known through proclamation and service ministries, beyond the borders of its own parish, as it spends to maintain itself. Paying the preacher, the fuel bill and the mortgage are usually matters of major concern!

It is unfortunately true that the average United Methodist Church spends more on pastoral ministry than it spends on Kingdom building. We must admit that money spent on pastoral ministry is money spent for ourselves. Many pastors function more like the court chaplain the kings once maintained: to marry, bury and baptize; and woe be unto the pastor who, for reasons of conscience, refuses to perform one these priestly functions. He is there, not necessarily to prick our conscience or challenge our complacency, but to speak comforting and encouraging words.

Some of these accusations of the church are unjustified but some of them are true. If they are true, there must be some valid reason why this is so. One of the reasons is that the local church has been relegated to a very insignificant role in this business of worldwide witness. It is looked upon, primarily, as a source of income and manpower to fill the ranks of the mission agency—a prime source of personnel recruitment and funds—and this is most regrettable.

Seldom is the local church looked to to provide much input so far as mission planning, strategy and decision making are concerned. They do not have much of a consultative role. Now, it may be true that there are few people in the local church with enough information or grasp of the issues affecting the mission program to offer useful advice. There may be times, however, when the homey wisdom of an auto mechanic or carpenter or farmer might help shape mission policy. What may be needed is a zeal for the task and common sense. Too often the layperson is asked to serve on a mission board because he or she has a little money or has been faithful to the programs and policies of the institution.

Certainly it is interesting to note how few local church members are in policy making positions. Not many mission agency executives have had broad pastoral experience. Most mission professors are drawn from the ranks of missionaries. Few can boast of long pastoral or local church experience.

It is my feeling that mission boards, both denominational and independent, have contributed to this situation of the local church having lost its vision for missions. For example, mission policies and programs are developed on a broad scale. When we talk about the church and its mission in the world we are usually taking about the church universal not the church local. Gordon McDonald, pastor of Grace Chapel in Lexington, Massachusetts, addressing the Urbana '81 Missionary Conference, said:

> "I want to lovingly confront you with the notion that your commitment to world evangelization must ultimately be set in a congregational context."

Jonathan Chao in, *Let The Earth Hear His Voice*, says,

> "We need a deeper understanding of the local church— the assembly of God's people in a specific place."

Perhaps this is one reason why mission policies often go wrong. They need to be more local church oriented. The local church, as we have said, has been treated as little more than a supplier of funds and personnel. The mission agencies have, at times, perhaps unintentionally, been patronizing. "The job is too big for you. Send us your money and your young people and we will get them to the field."

Now, we may be overstating the case but there does seem to have been a lack of effective relationship between the mission agency and the local church. We must remember that it was the church at Antioch which sent out Barnabas and Saul, not the Antioch/Cyprus Missionary Society or ACMS! (Of course it would have been better if I could have thought of a title that was an acronym!) It must be remembered that the local church can exist without the mission agency but the mission agency cannot exist without the local church. In a very real sense, the mission board or society is not the sending agency, it is the servicing agency. The church is the sending agency. As Andrew Murray points out in, *Key to The Missionary Problem,* "It is the church which is the connecting link between a dying world and a dying Savior."

This is not to say that we do not need the mission agencies. On the contrary, in our complex world of visas, passports, travel permits, world monetary problems, the training of missionaries and the conveying of information between the missionary on the field and the praying church at home, they are virtually indispensable. But, it should always be remembered that the mission agency is an extension of the local church, not a substitute; not, "rather than" but in addition to.

It is not my desire or intention to saddle the mission agency with all the blame for the present lack of mission involvement and vision on the part of the local church. On the contrary, we must admit that a lion's share of responsibility for this situation rests with the local church and its pastors. Again, as Andrew Murray points out,

"If missions are the chief end of the church then the
chief end of the ministry ought to be to equip the
church for this."

I guess what I am appealing for is closer cooperation between the
local church and the mission agencies. This would have many advan-
tages for all concerned, the mission agency, the local church and, most
especially, for the missionary.

To this end, it would help immeasurably if the missionary candidate
was commissioned in the local church with the laying on of hands by
the local church authorities with representation from the mission
agency, whether denominational or independent, present and participating. As George Peters points out,

"...the proper exercise of this Biblical principle by
the churches would do more to boost the morale of
our missionaries and the flow of missionary candi-
dates than many other factors combined. Our young
people should realize that not only does, 'my church
go with me, but my church goes in my person, stands
with me, prays with me, sacrifices with me, and
underwrites my support.' The challenge would
become inescapable. Here is the church's real opportunity, responsibility and challenge to herself and her
young people. Laying on of hands is not a favor we
extend, but a divine authority we exercise and
responsibility we assume. A church should think
soberly before it performs it."

Peters goes on to say,

"Such relationship of mutual identification and loyal
representation would certainly do much for missions.
It would prove rewarding for the church, the missionary and the work. It would involve the church
more directly in missions and would bind the missionary to the church in a healthy and bolstering
manner. He or she would feel neither independent
nor forsaken, knowing that he or she has a home
church that has gone with him or her into the field
while the church would know that she is actively
involved in mission in a representative manner.

> Returning from the field, the missionary would find
> a home for his family and a place where they could
> enrich their life while making a contribution to the
> home church." (Peters, *A Biblical Theology Of
> Missions*: pages 221-2)

So strongly does John Perkins of *Voice of Calvary* believe in this principle that he urges it even for short term volunteers. Every volunteer should be commissioned by the local church so that he would recognize that,

> "he is not a lone ranger, but is being sent out by and
> supported by the local church and, therefore, is
> responsible to report back to the local church the
> account of his experience and in this way the whole
> church shares in the missionary's joys and pains. The
> volunteer becomes the eyes and ears of the church
> among the poor." (John Perkins, *With Justice for All*,
> page 84)

When H. P. Speeks and John Perkins and their families were to start a new ministry they were commissioned by the local fellowship in Mendenhall, Mississippi and sent off to Jackson, Mississippi—a distance all of forty miles!

Certainly such a relationship would make for greater confidence, respect, loyalty and accountability on the part of all parties involved in the task of worldwide witness.

It is also possible, and I know that it borders on heresy to even suggest it, but in some situations the missionary could go directly from the local church to the field in one of the many tentmaker ministries that are open today, bypassing the agency altogether. This might be one means of avoiding the hostility and suspicion that surrounds the career missionary who goes out under a board or agency.

It may also be one means of solving the problem of the less than aggressive recruitment policy on the part of our own Board of Global Ministries. If the officially designated agency isn't going to do it, the local church may have to. A few churches and local fellowships already have become sending agencies. Organizations such as WEGO of Tyler Street Church in Dallas or Christian Lay Ministries based in Junaluska, North Carolina are but a few.

How can the local church become the agency for reconciliation that God wants it to be? I want to suggest several things. They have not to do with organizational procedures or structures but about principles that must be followed.

1. We Must be Convinced that Christ and Christ Alone is Mankind's Hope of Eternal Salvation

Michael Green says,

> "Most sections of the modern church are far from convinced that it matters much whether you have Christ or not...God is far too nice to damn anyone." (*Let The Earth Hear His Voice*, page 159)

We just must admit that if many of the leaders of our church are theological universalists then many of the members are practical universalists!

We must hold the same conviction as Peter, and with the same reckless abandon, when he declared, "Salvation is found in no one else, for there is no other Name under heaven given to men by which we must be saved." Acts 4:12 NIV.

2. We Need a Clear Understanding of the Nature and Purpose of the Church

The purpose of the church is to be the same as the purpose of God and all the activity of God, that we know of, since the Fall, has been aimed at reconciliation. From Genesis to Revelation a seeking God is portrayed. Whatever He has revealed Himself to be, we are to be, for we were created in His image. We understand this concept when we talk about the Church being the Body of Christ. If He came to seek and to save the lost, we are to be about the same business. It is strange that, generally, we agree that this is the business of the church yet in the average church so little attention is given to it.

3. We Need a Vision of and Burden for the Lost

Perhaps one of the greatest mission motivational passages in the Bible is found in Matthew 9:35, "and when He saw the crowds He had compassion on them because they were harassed and helpless, like sheep without a shepherd." We, too, need to see the world through the eyes of Christ not just their suffering and hunger but their lostness! I do not want to get involved in an exegesis of this passage but I cannot help observing that it was their lostness, "like sheep without a shepherd", not just their hunger and suffering that motivated Christ to have compassion on them.

If we had a vision of the lost it would galvanize us to greater commitment and sacrificial action. We would be possessed of a divine urgency. There would be little time for argument about methods or policies but a consuming desire to get on with the job!

When I graduated from high school I received a Bible as a gift. On the flyleaf I wrote the following words of Charles Inwood. The only thing I would change today are the figures, for in my lifetime they have more than doubled.

> "The sob of a thousand million of poor heathen sounds in my ear, and moves my heart; and I try to measure as God helps me, something of their darkness, something of their blank misery, something of their despair. Oh think of these needs! I say again, they are ocean depths; and, beloved, in my Masters Name, I want you to measure them, I want you to think earnestly about them, and I want you to look at them, until they appall you, until you cannot sleep, until you cannot criticize."

Eric Alexander, in his Bible studies at Urbana '81 reminds us that China Inland Mission, now Overseas Missionary Fellowship, was born out of the agony in the heart of Hudson Taylor over worship divorced from missions. In June 1865 while worshipping in Brighton England, he was unable to bear the sight of a congregation of a thousand or more rejoicing in their own security while millions were perishing.

4. The Burden of the Prayer Life of the Church Should be for Harvesters

It should startle us into alertness to note that immediately after seeing the multitude and being moved to compassion for them He said to His disciples, "The harvest is plentiful, the workers are few, pray the Lord of harvest to send out workers into His harvest field." Matthew 9:37,38

Surely, in obedience to our Lord, this petition should occupy a large place in the prayer life of every church. To my own shame I must admit that, at this point, I failed, miserably, the congregations that I served.

Is it possible that the spiritual maturity of any congregation can be measured by the harvesters it produces? Churches often complain that they never see a real live missionary. That would never happen if they were producing them.

The prophet Joel said that, "Your old men will dream dreams." I have a dream. I dream of every local United Methodist Church producing its own missionary! If we did, that would mean 38,000 missionaries or about the total number of career missionaries from all agencies in the US! Impossible you say? I would remind you that the Christian and Missionary Alliance church has one missionary for every 125 baptized members. The Assemblies of God of Finland has one missionary for every 45 members. The Moravian Church, at its height, had one missionary for every 38 members. No wonder John Wesley was impressed by them! If we did as well the United Methodists would have a 230,000 missionaries. Unfortunately, at present, we have one missionary for about every 25,000 members. Even if you count the United Methodists who are serving under independent boards we only have about one missionary for every five or six thousand members.

5. The Local Church Needs to Reorder its Priorities

Worldwide witness must be our number one priority. We must admit that it is not very high on the agenda of the average church. Consideration of the mission budget usually is left until last, after we have taken care of all local expenses. Ought we not, as pastors be embarrassed that more is spent to maintain us than is spend for witness and service both within and beyond the borders of our parish?

Buildings, for many congregations, have become the number one priority. After we get the building paid for, then we can turn our attention to missions. How often have I been called for a Missions Conference and told, "Now that we have the mortgage paid we would like to become more involved in missions." That's getting the cart before the horse. Should not missions have been higher on the agenda than the building? Inordinate interest in buildings may be the primrose path down which the devil has led the modern church. It grieves me to see some of the more evangelical denominations becoming so enamored of buildings because buildings seem to be an indication of success.

Paul Kaufman, in his book, China: The Emerging Challenge, points out that it was only after the communists had removed all their pastors and closed all their churches that the church in China really began to grow.

Certainly it is interesting to note that the church at Antioch did not have a church building when God spoke to them and said, "Set apart for me, Barnabas and Saul for the work to which I have called them." Acts 13:2. Not very practical on their part to have sent out missionaries before they got their building erected and paid for!

We need to recognize that our resources are not for the enhancement of the local congregation but for the advancement of the Kingdom; not for the enlargement of the building but for the enlargement of the borders of the Kingdom of God.

6. We Need to Talk Missions to Two Groups— the Children and the Men

I believe we will never build a strong missions church until more attention is paid to these two groups. In past years they have been neglected. Have you ever noticed how little mission material there is for children and almost none for men? Until work crusades and witness teams were started men had virtually been excluded from missions. It has been the women's sphere of responsibility. Now, thank God, that is changing.

Flo Martin, former Good News Board member and Director of Christian Education at the Wilmore Church said, at the Vacation Bible School program, when talking about the mission emphasis this year said, "What better time than now to plant a passion for missions in these little children!"

7. We Need to Pray for that Power that Enables

It seems quite clear that the imparting of the Holy Spirit was not to make me feel good or give me some special gift for my satisfaction but for the purpose of empowerment to witness "in Jerusalem, Judea, Samaria, and unto the uttermost parts of the earth." The ultimate purpose of missions is to glorify God. Our commitment, therefore, should be as total as was Christ's, "Who, though He was in the form of God, did not regard equality with God as something to be exploited, but emptied Himself, taking the form of a slave, being born in human likeness.

And, being found in human form, He humbled Himself and became obedient to the point of death— even death on the cross. Therefore, God also highly exalted Him and gave Him the name that is above every name, so that at the name of Jesus every knee should bend, in heaven and on earth and under the earth, and every tongue should confess that Jesus Christ is Lord, to the glory of God the Father." Philippians 2:6-11